Health Science Projects About
Your Senses

Robert Gardner

Science Projects

Enslow Publishers, Inc.

40 Industrial Road   PO Box 38
Box 398   Aldershot
Berkeley Heights, NJ 07922   Hants GU12 6BP
USA   UK

http://www.enslow.com

Library of Congress Cataloging-in-Publication Data

Gardner, Robert, 1929–
        Health science projects about your senses / Robert Gardner.
            p. cm. — (Science projects)
        Includes bibliographical references (p.   ) and index.
        ISBN 0-7660-1437-1
        1. Senses and sensation—Experiments—Juvenile literature. 2. Biology projects—
Juvenile literature. [1. Senses and sensation—Experiments. 2. Experiments. 3. Science
projects.] I. Title.
        QP434 .G365 2000
        612.8—dc21

                                                                00-010047

Printed in the United States of America

10 9 8 7 6 5 4 3 2

To Our Readers: We have done our best to make sure all Internet addresses in this book
were active and appropriate when we went to press. However, the author and the publisher
have no control over and assume no liability for the material available on those Internet sites
or on other Web sites they may link to. Any comments or suggestions can be sent by e-mail
to comments@enslow.com or to the address on the back cover.

Illustration Credits: Stephen F. Deslisle, pp. 26, 32, 37, 38, 42, 53, 57 (b), 61,
63, 96, 103; Enslow Publishers, Inc., pp. 14, 17, 20, 23, 24, 44, 47, 48, 49, 69, 76
(a, c), 100; LifeART image copyright 1998 Lippincott Williams & Wilkins. All
rights reserved, pp. 10, 57 (a), 76 (b).

Cover Illustrations: Jerry McCrea (foreground); © Corel Corporation (background).

Contents

*appropriate ideas for science fair project

*appropriate ideas for science fair project

Introduction

The science projects and experiments in this book have to do with your senses, with the ways you detect the sights, sounds, odors, tastes, and touches that reach your body.

You can learn a lot about your senses by doing experiments. Most of the materials you will need to carry out your investigations can be found in your home, a hardware store, a pharmacy, or a supermarket. For a few experiments, you may want to borrow an item or two from your school's science department. If the school's policy prevents your teachers from letting you take equipment home, you can probably carry out these experiments at school during free time.

For some of the experiments you will need one or more people to help you. It would be best if you work with friends or adults who enjoy experimenting as much as you do. In that way you will all enjoy what you are doing. **If any experiment involves the risk of injury, it will be made known to you. In some cases, to avoid any danger, you will be asked to work with an adult. Please do so. We do not want you to take any chances that could cause you injury or pain.**

Like all good scientists, you will find it useful to record in a notebook your ideas, notes, data, and anything you can conclude from your experiments. By so doing, you can keep track of the information you gather and the conclusions you reach. Using your notebook, you can refer to experiments you have done, which may help you in doing future projects. In some of the experiments, you will have to make some calculations. Therefore, you may find it helpful to have a calculator nearby as you do these experiments and analyze the data you collect.

Science Fairs

Some of the projects in this book may be appropriate for a science fair. Those projects are indicated with an asterisk (*). However, judges at such fairs do not reward projects or experiments that are simply copied from a book. For example, a model of the human eye, which is commonly found at these fairs, would probably not impress judges unless it was done in a novel or creative way. A model of the eye with a flexible lens that could produce images of objects at any distance from the "eye" would receive more consideration than a rigid papier-mâché model.

Science fair judges tend to reward creative thought and imagination. It is difficult to be creative or imaginative unless you are really interested in your project. Consequently, be sure to choose a subject that appeals to you. Before you jump into a project, consider, too, your own talents and the cost of materials you will need.

If you decide to use a project found in this book for a science fair, you should find ways to modify or extend it. This should not be difficult, because you will probably discover that as you carry out these investigations new ideas for experiments will come to mind—experiments that could make excellent science fair projects, particularly because the ideas are your own and are interesting to you.

If you decide to enter a science fair and have never done so before, you should read some of the books listed in the Further Reading section, including *Science Fair Projects—Planning, Presenting, Succeeding*, which is one of the books in this series. These books deal specifically with science fairs and will provide plenty of helpful hints and lots of useful information that will enable you to avoid the pitfalls that sometimes plague first-time entrants. You will learn how to prepare appealing reports that include charts and graphs, how to set up and display your work, how to present your project, and how to relate to judges and visitors.

Safety First

Most of the projects included in this book are perfectly safe. However, the following safety rules are well worth reading before you start any project.

1. Do any experiments or projects, whether from this book or of your own design, under the supervision of a science teacher or other knowledgeable adult.

2. Read all instructions carefully before proceeding with a project. If you have questions, check with your supervisor before going any further.

3. Maintain a serious attitude while conducting experiments. Fooling around can be dangerous to you and to others.

4. Wear approved safety goggles when you are working with a flame or doing anything that might cause injury to your eyes.

5. Do not eat or drink while experimenting.

6. Have a first-aid kit nearby while you are experimenting.

7. Do not put your fingers or any object other than properly designed electrical connectors into electrical outlets.

8. Never experiment with household electricity except under the supervision of a knowledgeable adult.

9. Do not touch a lit high-wattage bulb. Lightbulbs produce light, but they also produce heat.

10. Many substances are poisonous. Do not taste them unless instructed to do so.

11. If a thermometer breaks, inform your adult supervisor. Do not touch either the mercury or the broken glass with your bare hands.

1

Vision

The human eye is a magnificent organ. It enables you to see the world around you, to follow the path of a ball thrown to you, to read the print in front of you, to view the world's greatest art, and to see and do a zillion other things. However, without the brain to which your eyes are connected, you would see nothing. For, ultimately, the sense of sight is found not in your eyes but in the rear portion of your brain. It is there that you make sense of the images that form in your eyes.

It is the energy in light that makes vision possible. Photons, the smallest bits of light energy, enter the eyes and stimulate the sensory cells (rod and cone cells) in the eyes that respond to light. The photons that reach the eyes are reflected by, or emitted, from the objects seen. The eyes, despite what you may read in comic strips, do not radiate light. The photons that enter the eyes from visible objects are refracted (bent) by the eyes to form two-dimensional likenesses (images) on the back sides (retinas) of the eyes. The pattern of light in the images stimulate a similar pattern of sensory cells that send nerve impulses to the brain.

The Eye's Anatomy

Figure 1 is a diagram of an eye that has been divided along a horizontal plane. (You are looking at a cross section of the eye.) The eye is basically a sphere with what looks like a smaller sphere projecting from its front side.

The interior of the eye is divided into two parts. The space in front of the lens is filled with a watery fluid called the *aqueous humor*. The larger space behind the lens contains a somewhat thicker liquid known as the *vitreous humor*. The vitreous humor is enclosed in a thin membrane that fills the bulk of the space within

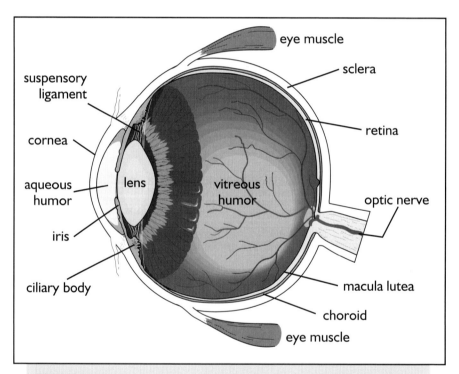

Figure 1. A diagram of the eye reveals a structure somewhat similar to a camera. Both have a lens. Images in a camera form on the film at the back of the camera. In the eye, images fall on the retina. A camera has a shutter that opens to allow light to enter. The eye has an iris with an opening in its center (the pupil) through which light enters the eye.

the eyeball. It maintains the eye's spherical shape in the same way that pressurized air keeps a basketball distended.

The eye has three separate coats. The outer coat is the white of the eye, or *sclera*. It covers five sixths of the eyeball. It is a firm, thick, fibrous membrane that protects the delicate parts of the eye that lie within it. The front part of the sclera, the part that bulges forward and covers one-sixth of the eyeball, is called the *cornea*. It is transparent so that light can enter the eye.

Look closely at your eye's cornea in a mirror. You may be able to see your own image in your cornea. The cornea is so smooth that it can reflect light just as a curved (convex) mirror does.

There are six muscles outside each eye that are attached to the sclera and to the skull. These muscles hold the eye in its socket and allow you to move your eyes in various directions.

The middle coat, or *choroid*, is a thin, dark membrane that lines the inner surface of the sclera. Just behind the edge of the cornea, the choroid folds inward like a ruffle to form part of the ciliary body. The ciliary body also contains the ciliary muscle, which is attached to the suspensory ligament. When the ciliary muscles contract, the suspensory ligament is less taut and the lens becomes more convex (rounder). When the ciliary muscles relax, the tension on the suspensory ligament increases and the lens becomes less convex.

The lens itself has a yellowish tint so that it acts as a light filter as well as a lens that refracts (bends) light. Were it not for our yellow-tinted lenses, we would be able to see a good portion of the ultraviolet light that is absorbed by the lens.

The front part of the eye's middle coat is the *iris*. It is the circular disk that gives an eye its color—blue, green, gray, brown, or black. At the center of the iris is a circular opening, the *pupil*, which allows light to pass from the cornea to the lens. The size of the pupil is controlled by muscles in the iris that can increase or reduce its size.

The eye's innermost coat is the *retina*. It contains the receptor cells—rod and cone cells—that respond to light. The light that forms images on the retina stimulates these cells, which send nerve impulses to the brain along the optic nerve. At the center of the retina, about 2 mm from the point where the optic nerve enters each eye, is a region known as the *macula lutea*. Images formed on this part of the retina can be seen very clearly. When you read, your eyes move so that images of the words fall on the center of the macula lutea where the *fovea centralis* is located. Here, in the fovea centralis, each cone cell is connected to a single nerve fiber that carries impulses to the brain's occipital lobe. The occipital lobe is located in the lower, back portion of the brain. In other parts of the retina, several cone or rod cells are connected to a nerve fiber leading to the brain.

1-1*
Forming Images

When light enters the eye, it is refracted (bent) as it passes through the cornea, lens, and the fluids that fill the eyeball. You can see that light is refracted as it passes from one substance to another quite easily. Simply put a pencil in a clear glass filled with water. Notice how the pencil appears to be broken at the point where it enters the water. Light from the pencil that passes through the water before entering the air is bent as it leaves the water. Light from the top of the pencil moves only through air and is not bent.

Things you will need:

- pencil
- clear glass filled with water
- magnifying glass (convex lens)
- room with a window through which a distant scene can be seen
- a friend
- white index card
- ruler
- lightbulb
- a second lens, more or less convex than the first one

Actually, the light from the pencil that travels through air is bent, but not until it enters your eyes. There, like all light, it is bent as it passes through your eye.

To see how your eye refracts light to form images on your retina, you can use a magnifying glass (a convex lens) to represent the lens in your eye. The lens can be used to form images of objects outside, such as trees and buildings, that you can see through the window of a room. Stand next to a wall opposite the window. The images will be clearer if you turn off any lights in the room that may be on. Have a friend hold an index card against the end of a ruler (see Figure 2a). The card represents the retina of an eye. Move the lens back and forth along the ruler in front of the card. At some point, light passing through the lens will produce a clear, sharp image of a distant scene that you can see through the window. Is the image right-side-up or upside-down?

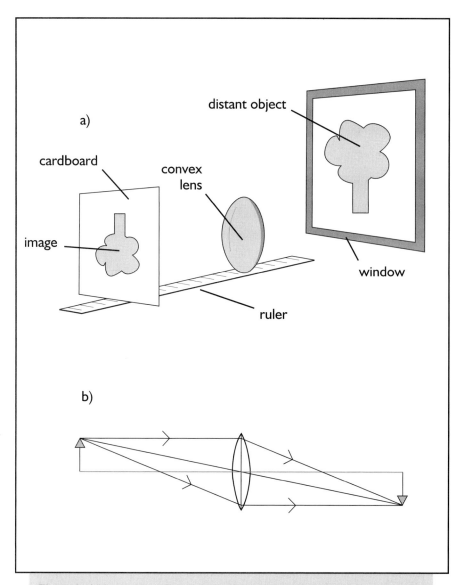

Figure 2. a) Use a convex lens to form an image on a card. b) Light rays from the top of an object (arrow) are shown as they approach, pass through, and emerge from a convex lens. The rays are refracted by the lens so that they come back together to form an image. What is shown here for one point of light happens for every point of light reflected from the object. As a result, the image is a replica of the object. Its size, however, depends on the distance of the lens from the object.

When you have a sharp, clear image, what is the distance between the image on the card and the lens? Figure 2b shows what happens to the light rays as they pass through the lens. You can see the light rays are refracted and brought together (converged) by the lens to form an image.

Now repeat the experiment. But this time have your friend hold the card and ruler about a meter (3 feet) from a glowing lightbulb. Use the lens to form a clear image of the bulb on the card. What is the distance between the image and the lens?

Move the lens closer to the bulb in a series of steps. At each point, have your friend move the card until there is a clear image of the bulb. Do you reach a point where it becomes impossible to form a clear image of the bulb?

Slowly move this book closer and closer to your eyes. Do you reach a point where you cannot see the print clearly?

As you probably found, the distance between the lens and a clear image of an object increases as the object moves closer to the lens. How are you able to see objects that are both near and far with equal clarity?

When you focus a good camera, the lens moves farther out or farther in to produce a sharp image on the film at the back of the camera. Do our eyeballs lengthen when we look at nearby objects? Do they grow shorter when we look at distant objects?

Our eyeballs fit snugly into their sockets, and we do not see them bulge outward when we look at objects held close to our eyes. Consequently, it is not likely that the shape of our eyeballs change. How then are we able to see objects that are both near and far?

To examine another way in which your eyes might adjust for distance, you will need a second lens. Find one that is more convex (fatter) or less convex (thinner) than the one you used before.

Using this lens, again produce a clear image of a distant object on the white card. Is the distance between the lens and the image the same or different than it was with the first lens?

Use the same lens to produce a clear image of a nearby object on the white card. Is the distance between the lens and the image the same or different than it was with the first lens?

As you can see, lenses that are more convex produce clear images that are closer to the lens. Less convex lenses produce clear images farther from the lens. You cannot slip lenses that are more or less convex into your eyes every time you shift your gaze from near to far or from far to near. However, you can change the convexity of the one lens you have.

When you look at distant objects, your ciliary muscles relax. This increases the tautness of the suspensory ligaments and your lens becomes less convex. As you have seen, distant objects form images closer to a lens of a given convexity. The more convex the lens, the closer to the lens the images form. Reducing the convexity of your lens increases the distance between lens and image so that the image of a faraway object forms on the retina. Under what conditions would you want your ciliary muscles to contract and make your lens more convex?

In fact, your ciliary muscles allow you to adjust the convexity of your lens so that you can form clear images of objects at many different distances from your eyes. What evidence do you have that there is a limit as to how convex you can make your lens?

Exploring on Your Own

As you have seen, the images formed by a convex lens are upside down. Why is it that even though the images on our retinas are upside down we see a world that is right side up?

What is astigmatism? What is nearsightedness? What is farsightedness? What causes each of these disorders? How can lenses be used to correct these visual problems?

Investigate a type of surgery called refractive keratomy. Who would need this surgery? Why would they need it?

1-2
The Blind Spot

The optic nerve and the blood vessels leading to the retina enter the back of the eye at a point slightly to the inner side of the macula lutea (see Figure 1). At this point there are no rod or cone cells. Consequently, we should expect to find a spot in every normal eye where we are blind.

You can easily detect the blind spot in your eye. On a white index card, use a black felt-tip pen to draw an X and a solid circle, as shown in Figure 3a. Both figures should be about 5 mm (⅜ in) wide, and they should be about 7 cm (3 in) apart.

Close your right eye and hold the card at arm's length with the circle directly in front of your left eye. Keep your left eye focused on the solid circle as you slowly move the card toward your left eye. You will find a point where the X disappears. Turn the card upside

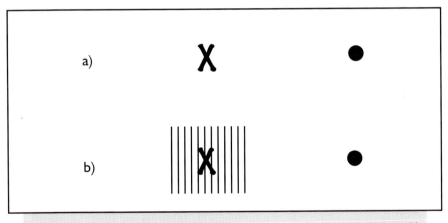

Figure 3. a) You can detect the blind spot in each of your eyes by drawing an X and a solid circle on a card. As you stare at the circle, slowly move the card toward your eye. The X will disappear at some point. b) What is different if you repeat the experiment but surround the X with vertical lines?

down and repeat the experiment with your right eye open and your left eye closed.

Can you explain why the X disappears?

Repeat the experiment, but this time use a card like the one shown in Figure 3b. As you can see, the X is surrounded by a series of vertical lines about 2 mm apart. What is different about the experiment when the X is surrounded by vertical lines?

1-3*

Measuring the Distance Between Your Blind Spot and Your Fovea

Your fovea centralis, where you focus images for clearest vision, is at the center of your retina. Your blind spot, where there are no light-sensitive receptor cells, is near the center of your retina. How far apart are these two small regions of your retina?

To find out, tape a square sheet of paper about 60 cm (2 ft) on a side to a wall or the door of a refrigerator. Use a felt-tip pen to make a small X (about 5 mm) at the center of the paper. Use the same pen to make a solid

black circle of about the same size as the X near the end of a white stick or ruler.

Have a friend sit in a high-back chair so that his right eye is exactly 1.0 meter (39⅜ in) from the X at the center of the paper and at the same height. The chair's high back will help your friend keep his or her head perfectly still. Ask your friend to close his left eye and focus his right eye on the X. By concentrating his gaze on the X, its image will fall on the fovea centralis.

While your friend focuses on the X, hold the stick so that the circle on the stick is close to the X on the paper. Ask your friend to continue to stare at the X as you move the stick with its circle slowly along the paper to your friend's right. Ask your friend to tell you when the circle disappears. When it disappears from your friend's vision, measure and record the distance between the X on the paper and the circle on the stick.

Repeat the experiment several times to be certain the results are consistent. Then repeat the experiment again several times as your friend focuses his left eye on the X with his right eye closed. This time move the circle slowly to the left until its image falls on the blind spot of your friend's left eye.

What is the average distance between the X and the circle when the circle's image falls on the blind spot in your friend's right eye? When it falls on the blind spot in your friend's left eye?

As you can see from the drawing in Figure 4, the distance between the points where the light rays from the X and the circle fall on the retina (which reaches the blind spot) form the base of a triangle, b, on the retina. The altitude of the triangle, a, is the distance from the retina to the lens of the eye. That small triangle is similar to another triangle whose base, B, is the distance between the X and the circle on the paper. The altitude of this larger triangle, A, is the 1.0 meter distance between the X and the eye of your friend.

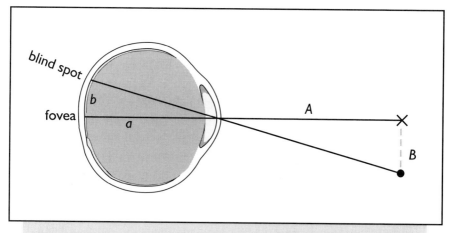

Figure 4. The large triangle with base B and altitude A is similar to the small triangle with base b and altitude a. The small triangle is inside the subject's eye. The base of the big triangle is the distance between the X and the circle when the circle's image lies on the subject's blind spot. The altitude of the big triangle is the distance from the X to the subject's eye.

Because these two triangles are similar, their sides are propor-
tional. Consequently,

$$\frac{b}{B} = \frac{a}{A}$$

Multiplying both sides of this equation by B gives us

$$\frac{b \times B}{B} = \frac{a \times B}{A}$$

Since $B \div B = 1$, we have

$$b = \frac{a \times B}{A}$$

Suppose you found the distance, B, between the circle and the
X to be 14 cm when the circle's image was on your friend's blind
spot. The distance from lens to retina within the eye, a, is approximately 1.5 cm. Your friend's eye was 100 cm from the X. Solving
for b, the distance between the blind spot and the fovea, we find

$$b = \frac{a \times B}{A} = \frac{1.5 \text{ cm} \times 14 \text{ cm}}{100 \text{ cm}} = 0.21 \text{ cm, or 2.1 mm.}$$

From the results of your experiment, what do you find the distance between the blind spot and the fovea to be? Is it the same for
both eyes?

Repeat the experiment, but this time you be the subject and let
your friend move the stick until the circle falls on your blind spot.
How does the distance between your fovea and blind spot compare
with that of your friend?

Exploring on Your Own

Is the distance between fovea and blind spot related to the size of a
person's head? Is it related to a person's age? To a person's gender?
Design experiments to find out.

1-4*
Binocular Vision

Because you have two eyes that are several centimeters apart at the front of your head, the images formed on the retina at the back of each eye are almost, but not quite, the same. When you look at something that is close by, both eyes turn inward toward that object, as shown in Figure 5a. The image falls on the fovea of the retina in each eye. The nerve impulses that go to the brain from the two eyes provide a fused image because they come from corresponding parts of each retina. The central portion of the image is the same in both eyes. However, the right eye sees farther around the right side of the object and the left eye sees farther around the left side. The fused image produced in your brain provides a three-dimensional view.

Things you will need:

- black pen
- Styrofoam cup
- pens of 2 different colors, such as red and green
- ruler
- red pen (or different color)
- a friend
- Ping-Pong ball
- pencils
- cardboard box about 15 cm x 15 cm x 30 cm long (6 in x 6 in x 12 in)
- cardboard
- sharp knife such as a skill knife
- two large nails

When you look at a distant object, both your eyes are turned to look straight ahead. As a result, the images of a nearby object do not fall on corresponding parts of the two retinas. Instead, as shown in Figure 5b, the image of the object falls on the right side of the right eye and on the left side of the left eye. As a result, you see two fuzzy images of that nearby object.

To see this for yourself, hold your thumb about 30 cm (1 ft) in front of your face as you focus your eyes on some distant object. How many fuzzy images of your thumb do you see? You know now why the images are fuzzy.

Next, focus your eyes on your thumb by turning your eyes inward. Why do you now see two fuzzy images of a distant object? Why are the images fuzzy?

Two Eyes Are Better Than One

You can easily convince yourself that we see a slightly different world with two eyes than we do with either eye alone. Use a black pen to draw a vertical line near the top of an inverted Styrofoam cup, as shown in Figure 6. To the right of that black line draw a series of vertical green lines at intervals of about 0.5 cm. To the left of the line draw vertical red lines 0.5 cm apart.

Hold the cup directly in front of your face. Hold it as close to your eyes as you can and still see it clearly. With both eyes open how many green lines can you see to the right of the central black line? How many red lines can you see to the left of the black line?

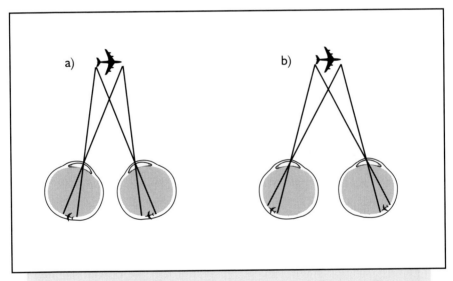

Figure 5. a) When you look at a nearby object, your eyes turn inward. The image of the object falls on corresponding points at the center of the retinas of both eyes. This produces a fused image in the brain. b) If your eyes are focused on a distant object, light from a nearby object will form fuzzy images on different parts of your two retinas. As a result, you will see two images.

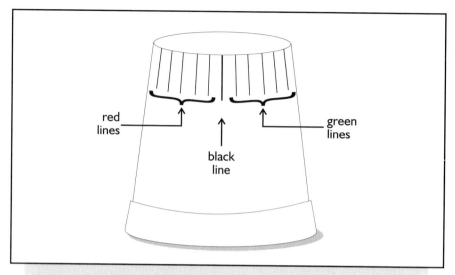

Figure 6. On one side of a black line drawn on a Styrofoam cup, draw green lines 0.5 cm apart. On the other side of the black line, draw red lines. Use the cup and lines you have drawn to find what one eye sees that the other does not.

Now close your left eye. How many green lines can you see to the right of the central black line? How many red lines can you see to the left of the black line?

Close your right eye. How many green lines can you see to the right of the central black line? How many red lines can you see to the left of the black line?

With which eye can you see farther around the right side of the cup? With which eye can you see farther around the left side of the cup? How is what you see with two eyes different from what you see with just one eye?

Depth Perception

A stereoscopic picture is made by taking two photographs of the same object at slightly different angles and then superimposing one on the other. Such a picture provides a sense of depth. Your eyes automatically provide a stereoscopic "picture." The large central part of an image falls on corresponding parts of the retinas of both eyes. Your right eye, as you have seen, sees more on its side of an object than does your left eye. Similarly, your left eye sees more on its side of an object than does your right eye. Your brain sees the central part of the image as a single image because the impulses come from corresponding cells of the retina. It then adds the extra parts seen only by the right and left eye to the central part to create an image that provides depth as well as breadth and height.

To compare your perception of depth using one eye or two, try the following experiments. Begin by playing catch with a friend using a Ping-Pong ball. Do you find it easier to catch the ball when you use two eyes or one?

Next, ask your friend to hold a pencil about 30 cm (1 ft) in front of you at about waist height. With both eyes open, try to touch the tip of the pencil with the tip of another pencil that you hold in your dominant hand. Now repeat the experiment with one eye closed. Then try the same experiment with the other eye closed. What evidence do you have that two eyes provide better depth perception than one?

Use a cardboard box about 15 cm x 15 cm x 30 cm long (6 in x 6 in x 12 in) to make a structure like the one shown in Figure 7. The box has narrow cardboard handles that can move along slots cut in the side of the box. The handles are used to slide two large nails along the bottom of the box. At one end of the box is a slot through which you can see the nails. Windows along the upper sides of the box allow light to enter so the nails are visible.

Ask a subject to look into the box with both eyes. He or she should see the nails at opposite ends of the box. Tell the subject to use the handles to move both nails toward one another until they appear to be at the same distance from his or her eyes. You can then measure the position of the handles relative to one end of the box to see how well your subject did. Then ask the subject to repeat the

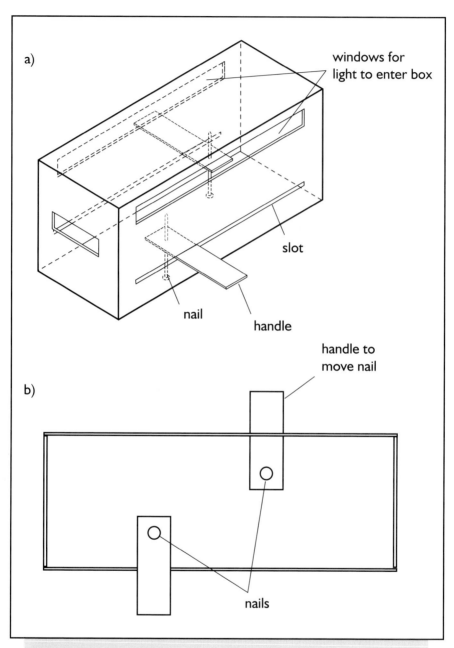

Figure 7. a) Diagram of box used to examine depth perception using binocular and monocular vision. b) Top view of box with top removed.

experiment with only his right eye open. Finally, have him repeat the experiment with his left eye open.

Try the experiment with a number of different people. What conclusions, if any, can you draw?

Exploring on Your Own

Roll a sheet of paper into a cylinder about an inch in diameter. Hold the tube up to your right eye while you focus both eyes on some distant object. Now hold your left hand at arm's length and slowly move that hand from left to right toward the front of the tube. At a certain point, you will see what appears to be a hole your left hand. Why do you think there appears to be a hole in the left hand? What happens to the hole if you close your left eye? Your right eye? How can you explain the hole in your hand?

Hold the tips of your two index fingers against one another about 30 cm (1 ft) in front of your face. Focus your eyes on a distant object. You will see what appears to be a small sausage between your fingertips. Move your fingertips just a little way apart and the sausage appears to be suspended in midair. Can you explain why?

Find out how filmmakers can produce movies with three-dimensional effects. Why haven't such movies become popular?

In addition to binocular vision, what other factors play a role in depth perception and estimating distances to objects?

Make a small hole through the center of a card with a pin. Remove the pin. Bring this book so close to your eyes that the print appears blurred. Now close one eye and hold the small hole in the card in front of your open eye. Why do you think you can now read the print through the hole?

Roll a sheet of paper into a tube. Look at a distant object with both eyes. Focus on some part of the object. Now hold the tube in front of one eye and again look at the same part of the distant object. Why do you think the tube improves your ability to see distant objects?

2

More About Vision

Your eyes are more than sensory organs that allow you to perceive light. There are cells in the eyes (cone cells) that respond to and differentiate among the various colors of light. There are also cells (rod cells), used primarily in dim light, that can detect only black and white.

Sometimes the images formed in our eyes can cause confusion or lead us to "see" things that are not really there, such as afterimages, aftereffects, and illusions. Some of these results occur in the eye; some take place in the brain.

In this chapter you will carry out experiments that will help you learn more about these elegant, yet mystifying organs that allow us to see both things that exist and things that only appear to exist.

2-1*
Rod Cells and Cone Cells

The retina of the eye contains a great many cells that respond to light. When struck by light, these cells respond by generating nerve impulses that travel along the optic nerve to the brain. There are two types of light-sensitive cells in the retina. On the basis of their shape, they are called rod cells or cone cells. The central part of the retina, the macula lutea, is rich in cone cells. As you know, the fovea centralis, where vision is clearest, contains only cone cells. This suggests that only cone cells are used when you read or look at the details of an object.

Things you will need:
- sunlight or bright light in a room
- dark or dimly lighted room
- a night with a star-filled sky
- a friend
- high table
- colored cards—red, yellow, green, blue, and other colors (optional)
- meterstick or yardstick
- people of different genders, eye colors, ages, athletic abilities, facial shapes, and some who wear glasses and some who do not

The outer, or peripheral, parts of the retina contain mostly or entirely rod cells. Rod cells contain a substance called rhodopsin, or visual purple. Rhodopsin breaks down into two smaller molecules in the presence of light. In bright light, most of the rhodopsin is quickly decomposed. During dim light it is produced faster than it decomposes and so its concentration increases.

Eyes in Darkness

After spending an hour or more in sunlight or in a bright room, go into a dark or dimly lighted room. How well can you see? Sit quietly in the room for a few minutes. Can you see any better now? What evidence do you have that the amount of rhodopsin in the rod cells of your eyes has increased?

After a few minutes, try to look at an object in the dark room. Do you see it better by looking at it directly or by viewing it through the sides of your eyes? Can you see the color of objects in the dark room? What do your observations tell you about the differences between rod and cone cells?

When you are outside at night, look directly at a dim star. Then look at it from the side of your eye. From which position do you see it more clearly? Can you explain why?

Eyes in Light

Peripheral vision is the ability to see objects that are to one side of you. In baseball, a good hitter must be able to keep the image of a fast-moving ball fixed on the centers of his or her retinas. A good basketball or hockey player, however, must always be aware of the position of his or her teammates so that accurate passes can be made. That person is often off to one side; consequently, the passer must have good peripheral vision. The player must be able to see from the "corners" of his or her eyes.

As you can see from Figure 8a, light that enters your eyes from the sides falls primarily on the periphery of your retina. What kind of light-sensitive cells are located in that region of the retina?

You can determine the extent of a person's peripheral vision. Ask a friend to sit at a high table with her chin on her fist. Tell her to stare straight ahead at a mark or a small object that is about two meters beyond the table.

Standing beside her, have her cover one eye while you slowly slide a colored card at eye level forward along a fixed measuring stick near her head, as shown in Figure 8b. The subject is to tell you when she first sees the front edge of the card.

Record the position of the card on the measuring stick at that point. Then ask her to tell you when she can identify the card's color. Again, record the position of the card when she can first identify its color.

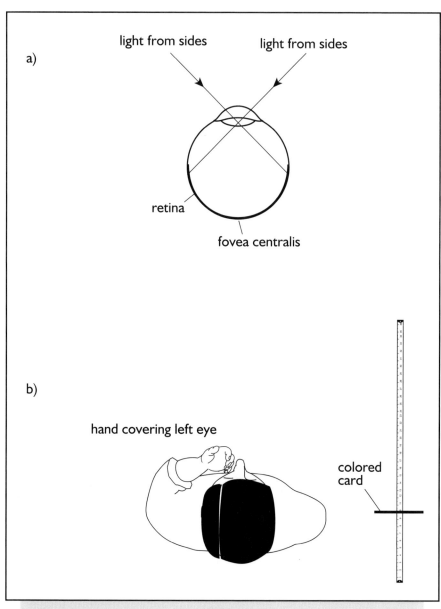

a)

light from sides   light from sides

retina

fovea centralis

b)

hand covering left eye

colored card

Figure 8. a) Light from the side of your body must fall on the periphery of your retina. What kind of receptor cells will respond to this light? b) An overhead view of an experiment to test for peripheral vision. A colored card is moved forward along a measuring stick until the subject can see it.

Repeat the experiment with cards of different bright colors— blue, green, red, and yellow, as well as black and white. Does the color of the card seem to affect the position at which the card is first seen? Does the color of the card affect the position at which the subject can first identify color? If it does, which color is detected first? Which color is detected last?

Repeat the experiment with the subject's other eye. Do both eyes seem to have the same peripheral vision?

Try the experiment with a number of different people. Does peripheral vision seem to be related to a person's gender? Eye color? Age? Athletic ability? Facial shape?

Do eyeglasses help or hinder a person's peripheral vision?

Design and carry out an experiment to measure the upper and lower limits of a subject's visual field. Include measurements of the field over which your subjects can see color.

Build a sphere to show the visual field of the average person. On that same field, draw the smaller area to represent the field in which color can be seen.

Exploring on Your Own

How can you use your data in Experiment 2-1 to determine the angle at which a subject can first see an object and the angle at which a subject can first see color?

Design and carry out an experiment to determine whether the rod cells we use to view objects in dim light are more sensitive to light of a particular color.

It's Where the Eyes Are

Suppose your eyes, like those of many animals, were on the sides of your head instead of in front. You would have a much wider field of vision. You would be much better able to see things to your side and behind you. Frogs can sit in water with only their eyes above the surface and see in a complete circle of 360 degrees.

Unlike many animals, primates, which includes humans, and some other animals such as bears and wolves, have both eyes on the front of their heads. Such an anatomy reduces the animal's field of vision. Are their any advantages in having both eyes at the front rather than on opposite sides of the head? If there are, what are they?

2-2*
Afterimages and Color

Stare at a bright, frosted bulb for a few seconds. Keep your eyes focused on the bulb; do not shift your gaze. Then turn away from the bright light and look at a light-colored wall. You will see a colored image of the bulb on the wall. Of course, there isn't any light there; it only seems to be there. The light you think you see is called an afterimage.

What is the initial color of the image? What happens to the color of the image as you watch it? Is the afterimage still present if you close your eyes? For how long does the afterimage persist?

Things you will need:
- bright, frosted lightbulb
- light-colored wall
- white paper
- ruler
- sheets of bright red, green, blue, white, and black construction paper; also (if possible) sheets of yellow, cyan (blue-green), and magenta (pinkish-purple)
- a dark room
- flashlight
- scissors

Can you block out the afterimage by holding your hand in front of the afterimage you see on a wall, or does the image then appear on your hand? What does this tell you about the actual location of the afterimage?

Once the afterimage disappears, which will take more time than you think, repeat the experiment. This time hold a sheet of white paper in your hand. After viewing the afterimage on the wall, shift your gaze to the paper. What happens to the size of the afterimage if you again focus your eyes on the wall? What happens to the size of the afterimage as you shift your vision from far to near? From near to far? Why do you think the size of the afterimage changes? Do you think the actual size of the image on your retina changes? What happens to the lens in your eye as you shift from near to far or far to near?

Allow time for your eye to recover and the afterimage to

disappear. Then stand close to the bright bulb and look at it again with only one eye open. Your other eye should be closed and covered with your hand because light can pass through your eyelid. Can you see an afterimage with the eye that was open? Can you see an afterimage with the eye that was closed? Based on the results of this experiment, does an afterimage form in the eye or in the brain? What makes you think so?

Allow time for your eye to recover and the afterimage to disappear. Then view the bright light out of the corner of one eye so that the image falls on the periphery of your retina, where there are only rod cells. Do you see an afterimage when the image of a lightbulb forms on the side of your retina? Can you explain the result of this experiment?

Afterimages of Complementary Colors

All the different colors of light can be obtained by mixing the three primary colors of light, which are red, green, and blue. For example, if you mix red and green light by shining both colored lights on the same area of a white wall, you will see yellow light. Mixing red and blue produces magenta (pinkish-purple). Cyan (bluish-green) can be obtained by mixing green and blue light. Mixing all three primary colored lights (red, green, and blue) will produce what you see as white light.

Two colored lights that produce white when mixed are said to be complementary colors of light. For example, red and cyan are complementary colors of light. When they are mixed, white light is seen. After all, cyan is a mixture of blue and green light, so when red light is added, the three primaries needed to produce white light are present. The color triangle in Figure 9 shows the primary colors of light at the vertexes with their complementary colors on the sides opposite the vertexes.

You can do an experiment to find the color of the afterimages you see after staring at a particular color. You will need to cut

36

squares 5 cm (2 in) on a side from sheets of bright red, green, blue, and black construction paper. If possible, obtain yellow, cyan (blue-green), and magenta (pinkish-purple) squares as well.

Place a blue square on a sheet of white paper. Place a second sheet of white paper beside the one with the colored square. Stare at the colored square for about thirty seconds. Then shift your eyes and stare at the blank sheet of white paper. What is the color of the afterimage you see?

Repeat the experiment with each of the other colored squares. What color are the afterimages of each of these squares?

Try the experiment with each of the colored squares again. As you stare at each of them, what do you notice about the edges of the squares?

Put a small red square on a larger blue square. Predict what the

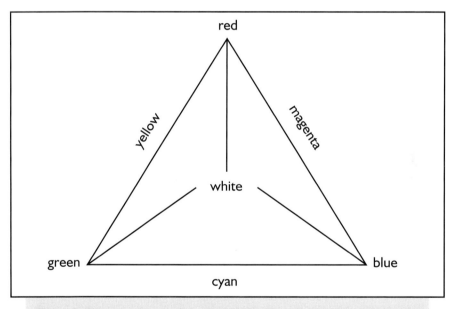

Figure 9. This color triangle for colored light shows the primary colors at the apexes and their complementary colors on the opposite sides. The colors along the sides show the color produced when the primary colors at each end of the side are mixed. White, at the center of the triangle, is the result of mixing all three primaries.

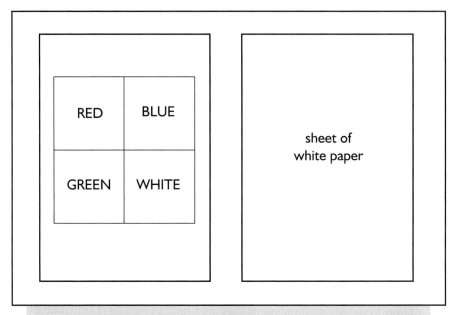

afterimage will look like if you stare at these squares for thirty seconds. Try it. Were you right?

What will be the colors of the afterimage that you will see when you stare at a small red square on a larger green square? A small blue square on a larger green square? A small green square on a larger magenta square? A small blue square on a larger yellow square? A small red square on a larger cyan square? A small black square on a larger white square?

Prepare colored squares, each about 3 cm (1.25 in) on a side, from pieces of red, blue, green, and white construction paper. Arrange the squares to form a larger square, as shown in Figure 10. Predict what you will see if you stare at the center of this multicolored square for 30 seconds and then turn your eyes onto a blank sheet of white paper beside the square. Try it! Was your prediction correct?

Positive Afterimages

The afterimages you have seen so far in this experiment are negative afterimages similar to those produced on the film in a camera. A bright white stimulus produces a black image. The image of the original bright object persists but the colors are opposite, or complementary, in the afterimage. Black objects produce white afterimages, white produce black, red produce cyan, and so on.

In positive afterimages, the afterimage is the same color as the object that produces it. To create a positive afterimage, let your eyes become adapted to the dark. Go into a dark room and stay there until your eyes have adapted to darkness. This may take 10 minutes or more. You will find that with time you are able to see more objects in the dark room. The rhodopsin pigment, or visual purple, in your rod cells is resynthesized after having been decomposed in bright light. As the concentration of rhodopsin in the rod cells rises, the capacity of the cells to respond to dim light increases.

Once your eyes have adapted to the dark, point a flashlight at your eyes. Turn the light on and look right at it for an instant and then turn it off. Turn your eyes toward a wall and you will see an afterimage. How does the afterimage compare with the light that caused it?

The light caused the rhodopsin in the rod cells to decompose. After the light was extinguished, the rhodopsin continued to break down, causing a positive afterimage.

After exposure to bright light, the rhodopsin quickly breaks down and we lose our ability to form positive afterimages. The rod cells, lacking rhodopsin, cannot respond. We are left with only cone-cell vision.

The chemicals in cone cells also break down, but they regenerate more rapidly than rhodopsin. To avoid cone-cell fatigue, we continually shift our eyes slightly so that the light in the images on the retina fall on different cone cells, giving previously stimulated cells time to recover.

Exploring on Your Own

Using colored pencils or pens, draw a picture of a flag that will have the flag of the United States as its afterimage.

Cone Cells, Color Vision, and Afterimages

Cone cells are located near the center of the retina directly behind the lens. They can detect color, but they do not respond to dim light. Only rod cells are stimulated by dim light, and rod cells can detect only shades of gray, not color.

According to one theory of vision, there are three types of cone cells, one for each of the primary colors of light—red, green, and blue. If light from a blue object enters our eyes, it is mostly the cone cells responsive to blue light that are stimulated. Similarly, green light stimulates primarily the cone cells sensitive to green light, and red light stimulates cone cells that respond to red light. Yellow light will excite both the red- and green-sensitive cone cells. Which cone cells, then, would be stimulated by a magenta-colored object? Which cells would respond to cyan?

Cone cells, like other sensory and muscle cells, become fatigued through use. When you look at something yellow, it is a combination of red and green light that is reflected to your eyes. Consequently, the cone cells that respond to red and green light are the ones that tire with prolonged exposure. When you then turn your eyes to view a white background, the cone cells sensitive to blue light are the predominant ones to respond because they, unlike the cone cells responsive to green and red light, are not fatigued. The afterimage, therefore, appears to be blue.

Using a similar argument, explain why the afterimages produced after staring at cyan and magenta objects are red and green respectively.

2-3*
How Eyes Make Movies Possible

As you have seen, the images that form on your retinas persist for a while. Even in normal light, it takes about one-fifteenth of a second for an image to fade. Movies are a series of still photographs shown at a rate of 24 or 32 pictures per second. For this reason, actors in movies appear to move normally.

You can use the persistence of vision to make a simple "movie" of your own. Make a series of stick drawings in the lower corner of a pad of paper. Draw each one as if you are see-

Things you will need:
- pad of paper
- pen or pencil
- sheet of cardboard about 30 cm (1 ft) on a side
- sharp knife or shears
- an adult
- well lighted picture
- colored pens or paint
- white 5-in x 8-in (13 cm x 20 cm) card
- tape
- spring-type clothespin
- wooden dowel or round pencil

ing it at successive stages in some activity, such as walking, running, throwing a ball, hitting a ball, etc. Make each drawing on a separate sheet. Once you have made the drawings, flip the pages in the proper sequence to see the stick figure in action.

On a somewhat different tack, ask an adult to cut a horizontal slit in a sheet of cardboard about 30 cm (1 ft) on a side. Stand near a well lighted picture. Close one eye and hold the cardboard sheet in front of the other eye so you can see part of the picture through the horizontal slit. Now move the cardboard rapidly up and down. Why are you able to see the entire picture through the moving slit?

Draw or paint a fish on one side of a white 5 x 8-inch card. On the other side of the card, draw or paint a fish bowl. Next, tape a spring-type clothespin to the end of a wooden dowel or round pencil, as shown in Figure 11. Place the card in the teeth of the clothespin. Now turn the card rapidly by rotating the dowel or

41

pencil between your hands. Why does the fish appear to be in the bowl?

Exploring on Your Own

Sometimes the action in a movie is shown in slow motion. How is it possible to make the action shown in a movie take longer than it normally would?

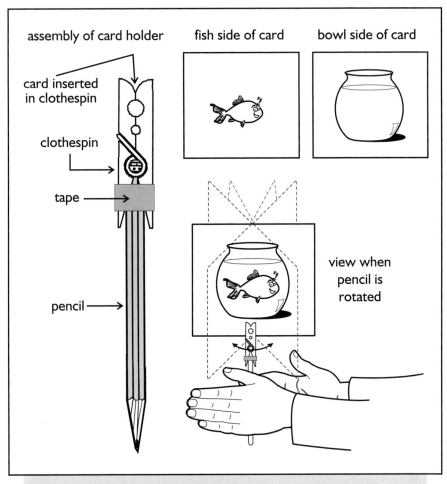

Figure 11. This experiment demonstrates the persistence of images on the retina.

2-4
Your Eyes as Cameras

The positive afterimages that form in your dark-adapted eyes make it possible for you to "take pictures" using your retinas as "film." To take such a picture, sensitize the "film" by sitting quietly in a totally dark room for twenty minutes while a friend waits outside. When the time is up, keep your hands over your eyes because bright light can pass through your eyelids and cause rhodopsin to break down. Your friend will lead you out of the dark into an area in front of a brightly lighted window where you will take the "picture."

Things you will need:

- dark room
- a friend
- brightly lighted window
- clock or watch
- color-blind person, if possible

You will need to hold your head very still, just as you would a camera. Remove your hands and open your eyes for one second. Focus your eyes on the scene through the window during that brief time, but do not move them. Then close your eyes and again cover them with your hands. Immediately tell your friend what colors you see. How do the colors in the "picture" you took compare with the colors in the real world?

How long does it take for the picture to fade from your retina? Does it change in any way other than intensity as it wanes?

If possible, have a person who is color-blind do the experiment. How does he describe the scene?

2-5
Aftereffects

In addition to afterimages, there are aftereffects. If you watch the water pouring over a waterfall for several minutes and then turn your gaze away, objects in your view will appear to move slowly upward.

Things you will need:
- a friend with a watch
- Figure 12

Stare at the slanted lines on the left in Figure 12a for about 5

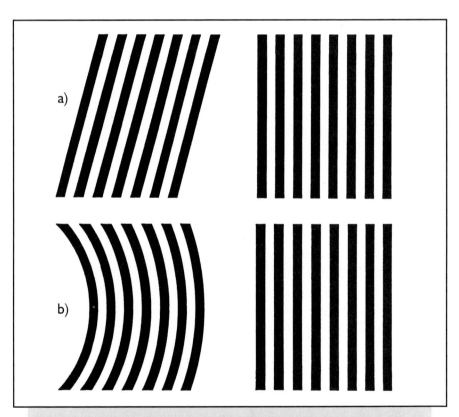

Figure 12. a) Look steadily at the tilted lines for about five minutes. Then look at the vertical lines. They will appear to slant in the opposite direction. b) Move your eyes along only the central portion of the curved lines for ten minutes. Then look at the straight lines. They will appear to curve in the opposite direction.

minutes. Have a friend with a watch let you know when that time has elapsed. Immediately shift your eyes to the vertical lines on the right. They will appear to tilt in the opposite direction from those you have stared at.

Next, look at the curved lines on the left side of Figure 12b for 10 minutes. As you gaze at it, move your eyes along the central portion of the curved lines. After 10 minutes, turn your eyes to the vertical lines on the right side of the figure. The vertical lines will appear to curve away from the lines you have been viewing.

Can you offer an explanation for these aftereffects? Can you design other ways to produce aftereffects?

2-6*
Illusions

Your experiments with afterimages and aftereffects have made it clear that not all you see is real. Illusions lead to the same conclusion. Through experience our brains have enabled us to learn how to deal with the images created within our eyes. For example, the images on our eyes are upside down; yet, we

Things you will need:

• pencil

• ruler

• white paper

• Figure 13

• black construction paper

• scissors

• glue

deal perfectly well with a right-side-up world. We have learned through experience to adjust to these images so that they make sense in the real world.

What do you think would happen if you wore spectacles that turned everything you see upside down so that the images on your retina were right side up?

Such an experiment has been done. At first, the subjects in the experiment found their upside-down world very confusing. After a few days, however, they adjusted and were able to turn their worlds around again and function normally. What do you think happened when they took the spectacles off?

Illusions provide us with false views of reality. Even when we know that we are viewing an illusion, we cannot change it. To see that this is true, draw a horizontal line exactly 10 cm long near the bottom of a sheet of paper. At the very center of this line, construct a vertical line exactly 10 cm long. Now look at the two lines. You know from your measurements that they are equal in length. But which line appears to be longer? Why do you think we perceive vertical lines as longer than horizontal lines?

Similarly, measure the lengths of the vertical "posts" in Figure 13. Even after your measurements, which post appears to be the

Figure 13. Which of these vertical posts appears to be tallest? Is it the tallest?

tallest? Which post appears to be the shortest? Can you explain why we perceive the posts in this illusion to be of different heights?

Finally, take a sheet of black construction paper and fold it in half twice. Draw a circle about 7 cm (3 in) in diameter on the folded sheet. Then cut out the circles by cutting through the four thicknesses of the folded sheet. Keep the circles together and cut out a quarter of the circles, as shown in Figure 14a. Next, glue the four three-quarter circles to a sheet of white paper, as shown in Figure 14b.

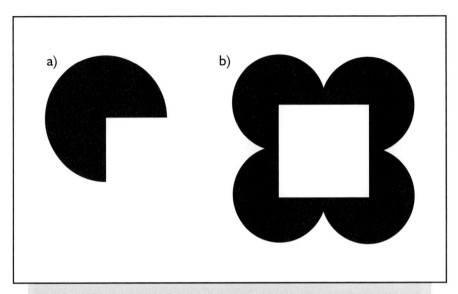

Figure 14. Cut four circles from a twice-folded sheet of black paper. Cut away a quarter of all four circles. b) Glue the remaining three-quarter circles to a sheet of white paper to make a square, as shown. The result is what appears to be a sheet of white paper covering parts of four circles.

You will see what looks to be a square sheet of white paper on a black background. In fact, a subject who has not seen what you have done would probably, at your request, try to pick up the "white paper."

Exploring on Your Own

Have you ever looked at a full moon as it rises over the horizon? It appears to be much larger than it does when it is well above the horizon. Is the moon really larger when it rises than when it is overhead? Design an experiment to measure the actual size of the moon as it appears on the horizon and when it is much higher in the sky. How do the sizes compare? Develop a theory to explain this illusion.

Try to develop explanations for the illusions shown in Figure 15.

Prepare some illusions of your own. Can you explain why your illusions produce the effects they do?

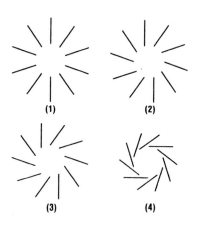

(1) **(2)**

(3) **(4)**

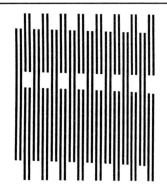

Hold this figure close to your eyes. You will see color between the lines.

You can probably see circles at the center of the straight lines in drawings 1, 2, and 3. Why don't you see one in drawing 4? Why do you see circles in drawings 1, 2, and 3?

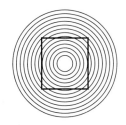

That's a square inside the circles. Why doesn't it appear to be square?

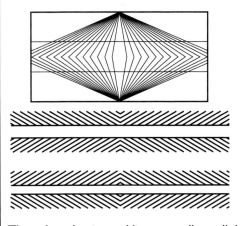

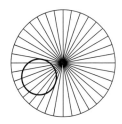

These long horizontal lines are all parallel. Why don't they appear to be parallel?

That's a circle crossed by radii inside a much bigger circle. Why doesn't it look like a circle?

Figure 15. Can you explain these illusions?

49

3

The Sense of Hearing

Your ears are the organs that enable you to hear. They allow you to perceive the sounds in the world around you, to locate the position of a singing bird, to recognize the sound of a familiar voice, to listen to a lecture, and to respond to the warning sound of a horn. However, without the brain to which your ears are connected by the auditory nerve, you would hear nothing. For, ultimately, the sense of hearing is to be found not in your ears but in the lower sides (temporal lobes) of your brain. It is there that you make sense of the sounds that reach your ears.

Sounds are caused by vibrating objects. Their vibrations produce pulses of pressure that can travel through gases, liquids, or solids. Most of the sounds you hear are transported to your ears by air.

Air, like all gases, is made up of tiny particles called molecules. Most of the air (78 percent) consists of nitrogen molecules. There are also oxygen molecules (21 percent), and small amounts of other gases such as argon and carbon dioxide.

Sound that travels through air is produced when a vibrating object pushes air molecules closer together, creating a region of higher pressure. That region of higher pressure then pushes on molecules ahead of it until the pulse of higher pressure reaches your ear.

Of course, a vibrating object produces many of these regions of high pressure as it moves back and forth. Consequently, a series of high pressure regions (compressions) with lower pressure regions (rarefactions) between them travel outward through the air. A series of compressions and rarefactions traveling through a medium such as air is called a sound wave. A diagram of such a sound wave is shown in Figure 16.

These sound waves, unless blocked, spread outward in all directions from the vibrating object.

It is important to realize that although sound waves move through air, the molecules of air simply move back and forth. They transport the wave, but they do not move with it. You can see the same thing if you watch a cork on the surface of a still pond. If you make some water waves by dipping a stick up and down in the water, the waves travel outward from the stick. As they pass the cork, you see the cork bob up with each passing crest and down with each trough. However, the cork does not move with the water wave. It simply bobs up and down in place. The same is true when a wave created by humans raising their arms travels around a sports stadium. The fans remain in their position, but the wave they create by raising their arms vertically travels horizontally along the crowd.

Most sounds do not consist of a single pulse but of many pulses closely spaced in time that are produced by a vibrating object. The vibrating object could be the string of a violin or cello, the oscillating air from a trumpet, the head of a drum, the motor of a car, or, more commonly, the vocal cords of another person. Most commonly humans communicate through spoken words, and it is the vibration of vocal cords that gives rise to the sounds we call speech.

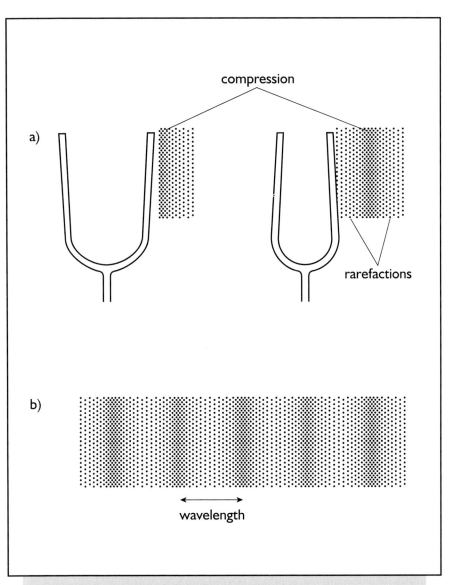

Figure 16. a) A vibrating object, such as a tuning fork, pushes air molecules together, producing a region of compressed air. Each compression is followed by a rarefaction (a region of low pressure) as the vibrating object moves in the opposite direction. b) A series of equally separated compressions and rarefactions traveling through air or another medium constitutes a sound wave. The distance between successive compressions or rarefactions is a wavelength.

The distance between successive compressions, or between successive rarefactions, in a sound wave constitutes a wavelength. The number of waves generated per second is the frequency of the waves. It is also, of course, the frequency of the vibrating object producing the sound.

Sound waves with a large frequency and a short wavelength are said to have a high pitch. Such sounds are made by someone singing soprano or striking the keys on the right-hand side of a piano. Sound waves with a small frequency and a long wavelength are said to have a low pitch. Sounds such as those made by a bass singer, a bass fiddle, or by striking the keys on the left-hand side of a piano have a low pitch.

When sound waves reach your ear, the changes in pressure that make up the waves cause your eardrum to move in and out with the same frequency as the sound. The changes in pressure needed to move your eardrum are very small. The human ear is incredibly sensitive. It can detect intensities as small as a trillionth of a watt per square meter. (That is less than the energy involved in a rustling leaf.) To understand what happens after a sound wave reaches your eardrum, you need to know the anatomy of the ear.

3-1*
Your Pinnae and an Old-Fashioned Hearing Aid

The flaps on either side of your head that you normally refer to as your ears are really only a part of your ears. Each of those flaps, consisting of skin, muscle,

Things you will need:

• radio

• large sheet of heavy paper, such as a poster

connective tissue, and cartilage that are attached to the sides of your head, are called pinnae. They are an important part of your organ of hearing. To see why, stand near a radio and either turn down the volume, or stand far enough away so that you can barely hear it. Now face the radio and use your fingers to turn your pinnae toward the sounds. What do you notice about the loudness of the sound when you do this?

A less direct way to see how your pinnae aid in hearing is to use an old-fashioned hearing aid. Long before there were battery-powered hearing aids, people who were hearing-impaired used a cone-shaped device that looked like a megaphone to help them hear better. You can make such a device by rolling a large sheet of heavy paper, such as a poster, into a conical shape. Hold the narrow end of the cone over one ear and turn that ear toward the radio you used before. Explain how the device improves your hearing.

Exploring on Your Own

On the sidelines at professional football games you often see concave-shaped disks that resemble the "dishes" used to pick up satellite TV signals. The devices are used by TV crews to pick up sounds from the field. How do these devices work?

If your school has an audio oscillator, use it to measure the range of frequencies that different people hear. Test people of different ages. What do you find? Does the sound level at which you play the sounds have any effect on people's ability to hear the frequency? Is there a frequency range that everyone can hear? If so, what is it?

55

3-2
Air Versus Bone as a Conductor of Sound Waves

Tap the tines of a table fork or a tuning fork against a wooden cutting board. Hold the fork near one ear. Tap the tines against the board again, but this time hold the handle of the fork between your teeth. By doing so you provide a bony pathway from the fork to your ear. How does the sound compare with the one you heard when the sound waves were carried by air? Where does the sound seem to be coming from?

Things you will need:
- table fork or tuning fork
- wooden cutting board
- cotton

Put cotton in one ear and again place the handle of the vibrating fork between your teeth. In which ear does the sound seem to be louder? Can you explain why?

Anatomy of the Ear and Transmission of Sound Within It

The human ear has three parts—outer, middle, and inner (see Figure 17a). The pinna attached to the side of your head collects sound waves and reflects them to the tube that leads to the eardrum. Sometimes you may cup your hand around your pinna to capture more sound when you have trouble hearing something.

The tube within the pinna that leads to the eardrum is called the *external auditory canal*. The inner end of this tube is surrounded by the temporal bone of the skull. Sound waves travel along this canal until they strike the eardrum, or *tympanic membrane*, which they cause to vibrate. The tympanic membrane marks the inner edge of the external ear. It separates the outer ear from the middle ear.

The air-filled middle ear lies within the temporal bone. It has a volume of less than half a cubic centimeter and connects to the top of the throat by means of the *eustachian tube*. The eustachian tube provides a passage that allows the pressure on both sides of the

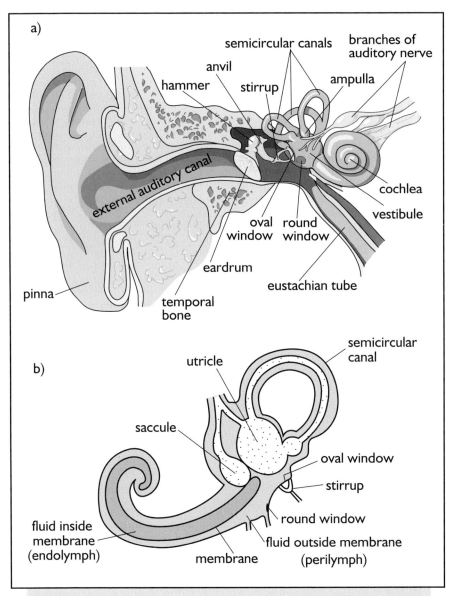

Figure 17. a) This diagram shows the outer, middle, and inner ear. The outer and middle ear are separated by the eardrum. The middle and inner ear are separated by the oval and round windows. b) The membranous labyrinth encloses a fluid (endolymph) and is surrounded by a fluid (perilymph) that separates the membrane from its bony surroundings.

eardrum to be equal. When you have a cold or an infection, the 3.6-cm-long eustachian tube may become blocked. This prevents equalization of pressure on both sides of the eardrum, causing reduced hearing until the tube is reopened.

Often, the tube will become obstructed with fluid in the pharynx (the region behind your tongue). Swallowing, yawning, or sneezing may clear the tube and equalize the pressure. If you have traveled by airplane, you may have had the experience of reduced hearing caused by unequal pressure between the outer and middle ear as the plane climbed to high altitudes or descended for a landing. Swallowing, yawning, or chewing gum may have opened the eustachian tube, allowing the pressure to equalize and your hearing to return to normal.

Within the middle ear are three bones—the hammer (*malleus*), the anvil (*incus*), and the stirrup (*stapes*). These three tiny bones form a series of levers that magnify the force on the eardrum about ten times. The hammer's handle is attached to the tympanic membrane. Its head is attached to the anvil. The anvil, in turn, is attached to the stirrup. The base of the stirrup rests on the oval window, or *fenestra vestibuli*, which separates the middle ear from the inner ear, or *labyrinth*.

The inner ear is a hollowed-out portion of the temporal bone. Within the labyrinth is a membrane, the *membranous labyrinth*, which encloses a fluid, and which is itself encircled by another fluid that cushions the membrane from its bony surroundings, as shown in Figure 17b.

The membranous labyrinth consists of a *vestibule* with two small sacs, the *saccule* and the *utricle*. Behind the saccule and utricle are three *semicircular canals*. These appropriately named tubes lie at right angles to one another and are connected to the utricle. One end of each canal is enlarged to form what is called an ampulla. All these structures are filled with fluid and nerve endings that send impulses to your brain.

The coiled, snail-like *cochlea* lies in front of the vestibule. The *basilar membrane* stretches across the cochlea, dividing it into two parts. The upper side is separated from the middle ear by the oval window. The lower side is separated from the middle ear by the round window, or *fenestra cochlea*. Another membrane—the *vestibular membrane*—divides the upper side of the cochlea into two parts so that the cochlea contains three coiled channels.

3-3*
A Look at an Eardrum and a Model Eardrum

Ask a parent, sibling, or friend to let you look into his or her ear. Gently pull on the pinnae to straighten the external auditory canal as you shine a pen flashlight into the ear. At the inner end of the canal you may be able to see the eardrum. If your subject's auditory canal is very curved, you may not be able to see the eardrum. If that is the case, try looking into the ears of another subject whose ear canal is straighter.

Things you will need:
- a parent, sibling, or friend
- pen flashlight
- tin can
- can opener
- scissors
- large balloon
- strong rubber band
- glue
- tiny mirror or a small piece of a broken mirror

To make a model of the eardrum, remove the top and bottom from a tin can. Use scissors to cut off the lower two thirds of a large balloon. Then stretch the bottom half of the balloon over one end of the can. Use a strong rubber band to hold the stretched balloon in place. Next, glue a tiny mirror or a small piece of a broken mirror to the balloon (see Figure 18).

Once the glue has dried, find a place where you can reflect a small patch of light from the mirror onto a wall. Now let sound waves strike the model eardrum. You can do this by speaking into the can. How does the "eardrum" respond to loud as opposed to soft sounds? How does it respond to high-pitched as opposed to low-pitched sounds?

How is your model similar to a real eardrum? How is it different from a real eardrum?

Exploring on Your Own

Extend your model to include a model of the middle ear. Extend it still further by adding a model of the inner ear.

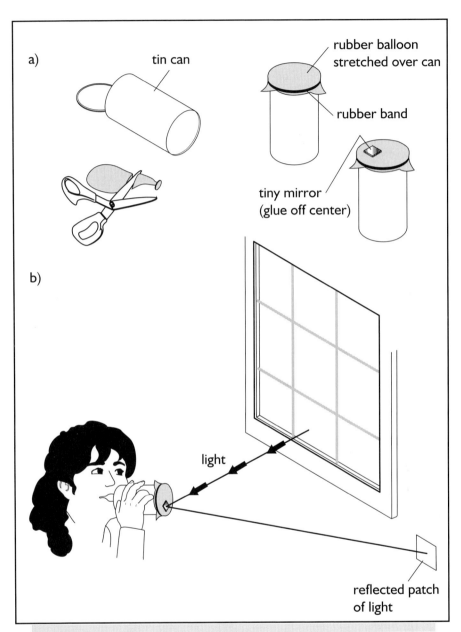

Figure 18. a) Prepare a model of an eardrum from a tin can, a balloon, a rubber band, and a tiny mirror. b) Produce sound waves that strike the "eardrum." See the magnified effect of the sound waves on the eardrum by watching the reflected patch of light on a wall.

From Sound Waves to Nerve Impulses and Hearing

When sound waves cause the stirrup to vibrate against the oval window, the fluid within the cochlea also vibrates. Thousands of hair cells of different lengths, together with supporting cells, are arranged along the basilar membrane. The length of the hair cells varies from about 0.13 mm to 0.28 mm. (A cross-section of the cochlea showing the basilar membrane is seen in Figure 19.) The tectorial membrane lies above these hair cells. When sound waves are transferred to the fluid in the cochlea, the basilar membrane also vibrates. Certain hair cells respond to a given frequency by vibrating themselves. As they vibrate, they move against the tectorial membrane. The motion generates nerve impulses that travel to the brain where the sound is perceived.

Shorter hair cells vibrate in response to high-pitched sounds; the longer hair cells respond to sounds of low pitch. The vibration of the hair cells produces nerve impulses that travel to the brain, where the sound is perceived to be of a particular frequency and loudness.

Although our vocal cords can only produce sounds ranging in frequency from 85 to 1,100 hertz (Hz), human ears can detect sounds with a frequency as low as 20 Hz and as high as 20,000 Hz. (The hertz is the unit used to measure frequency. One hertz is equal to one vibration per second.) Humans, however, vary greatly in the range of sound frequencies they can hear. Generally, our ability to hear high frequencies decreases with age, and many older people have difficulty hearing sounds with frequencies well above 20 Hz. Generally, people are most sensitive to sounds with frequencies of 2,000–3,000 Hz.

Other animals can hear sounds of much higher frequency. Dogs can hear frequencies as high as 50,000 Hz. That is why dogs will respond to the high-pitched sounds of a whistle that we cannot hear.

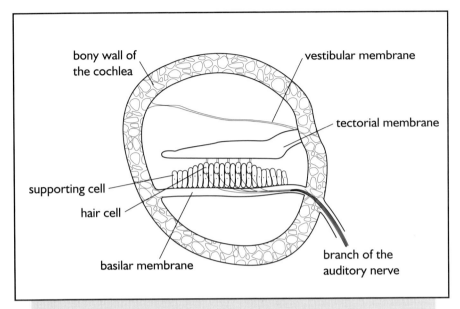

Figure 19. This cross-sectional view of the cochlea shows the basilar and tectorial membranes and the hair cells that connect to nerve cells from a branch of the auditory nerve.

Bats, who emit sounds with frequencies as high as 120,000 Hz, can hear sounds of the same frequency. In fact, they use these high-pitched sounds to detect the insects on which they feed. Sound waves produced by a bat are reflected from an insect's body. The fast-flying bat with its large pinnae can sense these sounds and follow them to the prey on which it feeds.

Some animals, such as elephants and large whales (finback and blue), make sounds that we cannot hear because the frequencies of the sounds are less than 20 Hz. For the same reason, we cannot hear the lower frequencies of the sounds emitted by earthquakes and volcanoes, some of which are less than one hertz.

Exploring on Your Own

Investigate how dolphins use the sounds they emit to detect their food and other objects in the sea.

Over what distance can large whales hear the low-pitched sounds other whales emit?

Are the organs of hearing found on the heads of all animals? If not, where else on the animals' bodies are they found?

The Inner Ear and Balance

The ampulla at the end of each semicircular canal contains a small organ known as the crista ampullaris. Rotation of the head in any direction, which may or may not be accompanied by rotation of the body, causes fluid in one or more of the semicircular canals to move. The movement of fluid pushes and bends hair cells that are embedded in the crista ampullaris. The hair cells then generate nerve impulses that travel to the cerebellum of the brain.

The cerebellum also receives nerve impulses from muscles, joints, the brain and spinal cord, as well as the semicircular canals. It also sends impulses to the muscles, other parts of the brain, and to various levels of the spinal cord. Although we are not consciously aware of it, the cerebellum enables the body to maintain balance and respond to changes in position.

Damage to the cerebellum results in lack of muscle tone, weakness, and loss of coordination due to poor muscle control that may prevent the victim from walking or talking.

3-4
Muscles, Eyes, and Body Balance

Although you are not aware of it, your muscles are constantly contracting or relaxing to maintain your balance. To see that this is true, stick a pin through the inside bottom of a Styrofoam cup so that the pin sticks out from the bottom. Then place the cup upside down on your head. Stand some distance from a sheet of paper taped to a kitchen cabinet or basement wall. Arrange a lightbulb so that the pin casts a shadow on the

Things you will need:
- pin
- Styrofoam cup
- sheet of paper
- tape
- kitchen cabinet or basement wall
- lightbulb
- a friend
- marking pen
- rope swing or chair that rotates

paper. Have a friend mark the position of the shadow with a pen and draw a line down the paper.

Try to keep the shadow of the pin on the line your friend drew. Try as you will, you will find it impossible to keep your body in the same position. The shadow will periodically move off the line.

You will find it even more difficult to maintain a steady balanced position if you stand on one foot. To avoid falling, the center of your body must be directly above one or more points of support (your feet or foot). If you stand with your left foot and the left side of your body against a wall, why can you not lift your right foot without falling?

Newton's first law of motion tells us that a body in motion remains in motion unless acted upon by an outside force. Consequently, if you set the fluid in your inner ear into motion by rotating your body, those fluids will continue to move in the same direction when you stop. As a result, you will feel as though you are still rotating. That is why you feel dizzy after turning in place a few times. Dizziness may also be accompanied by nystagmus—involuntary motion of the eyes.

Have a friend sit in a rope swing. (You can also do this experiment on a chair that rotates, but you will have to supply the force to make the chair rotate.) Turn the subject so that the two ropes wind around one another many times. Then release the swing so that the subject rotates as the ropes unwind. Once the swing has unwound, stop the rotation and look at the subject's eyes. Can you detect nystagmus?

Now have the subject wind the ropes as you sit on the swing. How do you feel after rotating? Do you sense that you are still turning? How does it affect your balance?

3-5

Do Your Eyes Play a Role in Maintaining Body Balance?

Your sense of balance, as you have read, is controlled to a large extent by the hair cells in your inner ear. These cells send nerve impulses to the cerebellum, which, in turn, cause contraction and relaxation of the

Things you will need:

- clock or watch with second hand or mode
- several people of different genders, heights, ages, athletic abilities, etc.

muscles needed to maintain balance. But do you think your eyes play a role in maintaining body balance?

To find out, stand on one foot in a large open space with your eyes open. Can you feel muscles in your leg and foot contracting so as to keep your body balanced? For how long can you balance on one foot?

Now close your eyes and try to stand balanced on one foot. For how long can you balance on one foot with your eyes closed? Do you find it as difficult to do in the dark with your eyes open? Do you think vision plays a role in maintaining body balance?

Try this experiment with a number of different people. Are some people better at maintaining one-legged balance with their eyes closed than others? If so, do these people tend to be athletes? Does height seem to have any effect on a person's ability to balance on one leg with eyes closed? Does age have any effect on a person's ability to balance on one leg with eyes closed? Are females better at one-legged balance with eyes closed than males? Do you detect any patterns that allow you to predict whether a person will have good or poor one-legged balance when his or her eyes are closed?

3-6*
Sound, Hair Cells, and Resonance

You have read that hair cells of different length on the basilar membrane of the cochlea respond to sounds of different pitch. The shorter hair cells respond to high-pitched sounds and longer hair cells to sounds with lower pitch. This is known as the resonance theory of hearing.

Resonance has to do with the fact that objects that vibrate have a natural rate (frequency) of vibration. An object's natural rate of vibration is determined by its mass, stiffness, and size. If a force acts on a vibrating object at a frequency that matches its natural frequency, the size of the vibration will increase. This response to a natural rate of vibration is called resonance.

Things you will need:

- construction paper
- scissors
- ruler
- tape
- cardboard
- a friend
- piano
- musical instrument other than a piano (optional)

To demonstrate resonance and the effect of frequencies, prepare a series of paper rings. Using scissors, cut 2.5-cm- (1-in-) wide strips of differing lengths from construction paper. The longest one should be about 50 cm (20 in) long. (Long strips can be made by taping shorter strips together.) The strips might be about 40 cm, 30 cm, and 15 cm (16 in, 12 in, and 6 in) long. Tape the ends of each strip together to make rings. Then tape the rings to a sheet of cardboard, as shown in Figure 20.

Shake the cardboard slowly back and forth from side to side at a very low but increasing frequency. The ring with the largest diameter will be the first to resonate. As you continue to increase the rate at which you move the cardboard back and forth, each ring, in turn, will resonate to a particular frequency. Will the rings also resonate to an up-and-down motion of the cardboard?

68

You can also demonstrate resonance using the strings of a piano. Ask a friend to push down on the right-hand pedal of a piano. If possible, look inside the piano when this is done. You will see that the dampers on all the strings are lifted when that pedal is down. Without dampers, all the strings are now free to vibrate. Sing a note into the piano or play a note on another instrument near the piano. Then listen to the piano. You will hear a sound from a piano string that is resonating in response to the pitch you sang or played. We say the piano string has been set into sympathetic vibration.

Use what you have learned in this experiment to explain why hair cells of different length on the basilar membrane respond to sounds of different frequency. How might you explain our ability to detect differences in the loudness of a sound?

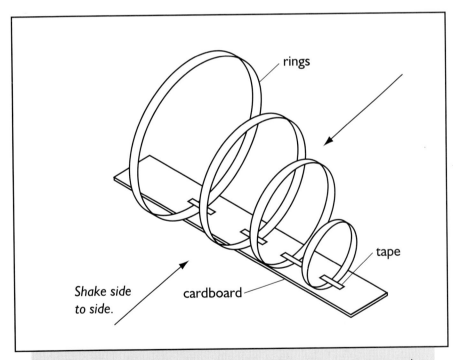

Figure 20. Resonating rings can be made from strips of construction paper that are taped to a sheet of cardboard.

Exploring on Your Own

Helen Keller, who became a well-known writer and a speaker, was born both deaf and blind. How did she learn to communicate?

Place open cardboard tubes of different lengths against your ear. How do the sounds you hear vary with the length of the tube? How are the sounds you hear related to resonance?

You may have heard that if you place a conch shell against your ear you can hear the sea. What is it that you really hear?

3-7
Keenness of Hearing

Ask a friend to sit in a chair in a very quiet room. Ask your friend to tell you when he or she can hear the sound of a ticking watch that you move slowly toward your friend's right ear. At what distance can he or she hear the watch?

Things you will need:

- a subject
- chair
- quiet room
- ticking watch
- radio
- a variety of different subjects

Repeat the experiment by bringing the watch toward your friend's left ear. At what distance can he or she hear the sound? Are the distances equal for both ears or does keenness of hearing in one ear exceed the other?

Repeat the experiment while a radio is playing soft music. Does the additional sound affect your friend's ability to hear the ticking watch?

Repeat the experiment with a number of different people. Is keenness of hearing related to age?

3-8
Locating Sounds

Seat a blindfolded friend in a chair in the center of a large carpeted room. (The carpet will dampen any sounds you make as you step around your friend.) Tell your friend you are going to tap two coins together at various positions around him or her. Your friend is to point to the position from which he or she thinks the sound is coming.

Things you will need:

- blindfold
- 2 friends
- chair
- large carpeted room
- 2 coins
- cotton

Then stand to one side of the subject and tap the coins together. Have another friend record how closely the subject is able to identify the position of the sound. Continue to move quietly to new positions at random and then tap the coins together. How closely can your friend identify the position of the sound?

Can the friend identify the position of the coins when they are tapped together at a point directly above the middle of his or her head?

Repeat the experiment when one of the friend's ears is plugged with cotton. Does loss of hearing in one ear affect the person's ability to locate sounds? If it does, can you explain why?

Hearing Tests at Birth

About 4 of every 1,000 babies suffer from some hearing disability. Consequently, most pediatricians recommend that infants be tested for hearing loss. Babies who cannot hear well are slow to speak and understand language. By detecting any diminished sense of hearing, babies can be fitted with hearing aids.

If they have total loss of this important sense, they can watch people using sign language and learn to communicate in that manner.

Since babies are unable to speak or write, their hearing cannot be tested in the usual way. One way to examine an infant's ability to sense sound is to place cuplets over the baby's ears and sensors on its head. The sensors can detect changes in brain waves that will occur when sounds are transmitted to the cuplets. Another method involves detecting the vibration of the tiny hairs along the cochlea of the inner ear when sound waves strike the infant's outer ears. In cases where hearing impairment is detected, treatment should begin by the time the baby is six months old.

4

Taste and Smell

Eating would be a rather dull affair were it not for our senses of taste and smell. As you will soon learn, taste and smell are closely linked to each other. But although taste and smell are closely related, there are differences between them. For a substance to be tasted, it must be a liquid or be dissolved in a liquid. To be smelled, it must be a gas.

Taste

Your sense of taste arises through taste buds embedded in the surface of your tongue (Figure 21a). In a taste bud, elongated cells with hairlike projections on their upper ends rest on supporting cells. Dissolved substances react with the hairs atop the taste receptor cells to produce nerve impulses that travel to the brain. It is within the brain that we perceive taste.

The nerve fibers from taste buds join the seventh and ninth cranial nerves before going to the brain. The tongue is also connected to the brain by fibers from the fifth, seventh, and twelfth cranial nerves.

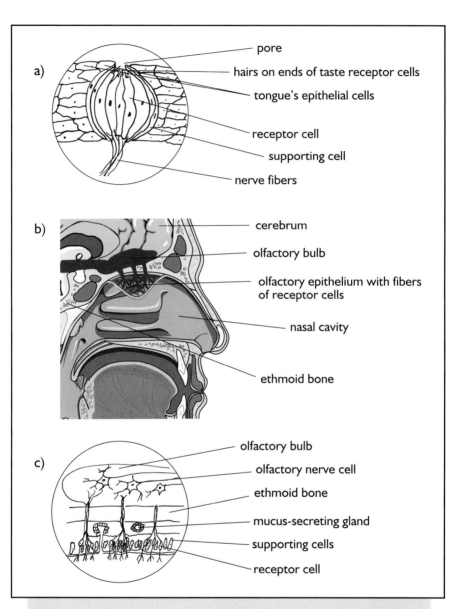

Figure 21. a) The surface of the tongue contains many taste buds, like the one shown here. b) Olfactory receptors are found at the top of the nasal cavity. c) Hairlike endings on the receptor cells are stimulated by gaseous molecules that dissolve in the nasal mucus and give rise thereby to odors. The nerve impulses are carried to the olfactory nerve cells in the olfactory bulb, and from there to various parts of the brain.

There are only four basic taste sensations—sweet, salty, sour, and bitter. Other sensations that we call taste are actually combinations of the four basic tastes with one another and with sensations associated with smell.

Smell

Although you can sense only four basic tastes, you can probably detect more than 10,000 separate odors. Most other mammals have a keener sense of smell than humans. Many police departments use dogs to track down criminals by following a scent left on the ground, or to search for bombs or drugs hidden in a building or airplane.

Deer have glands in their hooves. A baby deer can find its mother by following the scent left by her hooves. At birth, and for a week following, a baby deer emits none of the chemicals that provide a scent. Such an adaptation helps to hide the baby from predators. After the first week, a mother deer will lick away the baby's growing scent each time before leaving it alone while she trots off to forage for food. Many mammals recognize their young and other members of their group through distinct odors that they can detect.

A keen sense of smell is not limited to mammals. Many insects, who use their antennae to sense airborne chemicals, depend upon smell to survive. Pheromones (chemicals used to communicate) released by a female moth may be sensed by a male moth half a kilometer (⅓ mile) away. Ants release pheromones as they carry food back to their colony. Other ants can then follow the scent to the food source. Dogs and foxes urinate on rocks and trees. The scent of the urine is used to mark their territory.

Limited though our sense of smell may be, it grows even weaker as we grow older. Olfactory receptor cells, the cells sensitive to odors, weaken with time. As a result, many older people lose their keen sense of smell, so many foods seem to have less flavor.

77

The receptor cells that respond to odors (olfactory receptor cells) are located at the top of the nasal cavity, as shown in Figure 21b. Nerve fibers extend from these receptor cells through the skull's ethmoid bone to the olfactory bulb at the base of the front part of the brain. There they connect with other nerve cells that travel to various parts of the brain.

The olfactory receptor cells, which are embedded in the cellular lining of the nasal cavity, have hairlike endings that extend through the lining. These hairs are stimulated by odoriferous molecules that dissolve in the nasal mucus released by mucus-secreting glands.

Unlike taste, odors are difficult to classify because there are so many and they are often a mixture of different pure odors. One attempt to classify pure odors divides them into nine classes—ethereal, aromatic, fragrant, ambrosial, garlic, burning odors, goat odors, repulsive odors, and nauseating or fetid odors. Pure odors, however, are rare, and the terms used to describe them are subject to interpretation. This is evident from the fact that another classification of odors lists them as camphorous, musky, floral, pepperminty, ethereal, pungent, putrid, resinous, and spicy.

Odors do, however, stimulate memories. An odor often brings to mind a past event or experience even though the connection between the odor and the experience may not be recalled. Do you have memories that spring to mind when you smell a particular odor, such as a certain food cooking or the scent of a particular flower?

4-1*
Testing the Tongue for Taste

Many animals have taste receptors, but not all animals taste with their tongues. Butterflies, for example, have taste buds on their feet. Their tongues are long coiled tubes that they can straighten to extend in order to reach the nectar deep within a flower. The body of a catfish is covered with taste buds, while lobsters have taste receptors on their feet and antennae.

In this experiment, you and a friend will try to locate taste buds for four different kinds of chemicals—salt, sugar, quinine (tonic water), and a weak acid (vinegar). The experiment is best done near a sink so that solutions can be prepared and mouths rinsed frequently.

Things you will need:

- 2 friends
- a sink
- graduated cylinder or metric measuring cup
- plastic cups
- water
- salt
- sugar
- white vinegar
- tonic water
- drinking straws
- cotton swabs
- notebook
- pen or pencil
- several people of different ages and genders

Pour 100 mL of water into a plastic cup. Stir in small amounts of salt until no more will dissolve. In the same way, prepare a solution of sugar and water in another cup. To a third cup add 50 mL of white vinegar to an equal volume of water. Pour about 100 mL of tonic water into a fourth cup.

Begin by placing a drinking straw in each of the solutions so that you can draw a small amount of each liquid in turn into your mouth. Swirl each sample around so that you can taste it. Rinse your mouth with plain water in between samples to remove a previous taste. As you will find, the salt solution tastes salty, the sugar solution is sweet, the vinegar has a sour taste, and the quinine is bitter.

Have a friend taste each liquid in the same way.

Have your friend rinse his or her mouth with water before you start searching for the receptors sensitive to the salt solution. Similar rinsing should be done before each test to remove any taste left by the previous solution.

Dip a cotton swab into the salt water. Then use the swab to touch your friend's tongue at the places shown in Figure 22. Ask your friend to raise a hand when he or she can taste the salt. Some people will not taste anything until after the test is over. Then, when they close their mouths, they will be aware of a salty taste at some point or points on their tongues.

Have a second friend record the place or places on the tongue where your subject could taste salt. Use a minus sign (–) to indicate the subject experienced no taste at that location and a plus sign (+) to indicate a taste was detected. If, after the test, the subject tells you that the taste was more intense at one location than another,

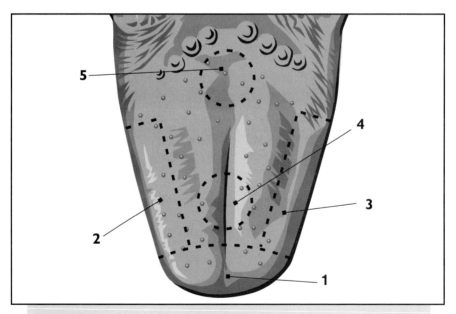

Figure 22. In which locations on the tongue (1, 2, 3, 4, and 5) can a subject taste the chemicals you are testing—salt, sugar, acid, and quinine?

record the location of the more intense taste with a double plus sign
(++).

After your friend rinses his mouth with water, repeat the experiment using the vinegar solution to locate the taste buds that respond
to sour. Where on the tongue are these cells located?

Again, after your friend rinses his mouth with water, repeat the
experiment using the sugar solution to locate the taste buds that
respond to a sweet taste. Where on the tongue are these cells
located?

Finally, use the quinine (tonic) water to test for the receptors
that respond to bitter-tasting substances. Where on the tongue are
these cells located?

Test your second friend in the same way, while your first friend
records the data. Then be your own subject. Have one friend test to
find the location of your different taste buds, while the second friend
records the data.

On the basis of your data, are taste buds for sour, salt, sweet,
and bitter spread evenly over the tongue? If not, where are taste buds
for each taste located on the tongue?

Suppose you had to swallow a bitter-tasting pill. Based on the
evidence from the experiment you have just done, where should you
place the pill on your tongue to avoid tasting it?

If possible, test a number of different people, including your
parents and grandparents. Do you find similar results when you test
other people? Does age seem to affect a person's sense of taste? Are
females more or less taste-sensitive than males? How can you tell?

Exploring on Your Own

Design and carry out an experiment to prepare a detailed map of the
regions of the tongue in which the taste buds for each taste are
located.

Your taste buds can detect the sweet taste of sugar. Can they
also sense the sweet taste of an artificial sweetener?

81

4-2*
Is It Taste or Smell?

It is bad enough to have a cold, but it is also a time when food seems to have no flavor. In addition to feeling "stuffed up," you cannot even enjoy the food you eat. In this experiment you will investigate how smell, as well as taste, is involved in recognizing a variety of foods. You can imitate a cold and repress your ability to detect most odors by holding your nose. If you taste a food with and without your nose closed, you can estimate how much of a food's flavor is due to your sense of taste and how much is due to your sense of smell.

Things you will need:
- grapefruit juice
- milk
- sugar
- vinegar
- water
- pickle juice
- onion juice
- small paper cups
- a friend
- chair
- blindfold
- notebook
- pen or pencil
- sink
- several people of different ages and genders

To carry out this experiment you will need a supply of grapefruit juice, milk, sugar solution, vinegar (mixed 1:1 with water), pickle juice, onion juice, and water. Pour a few milliliters of each liquid into separate small paper cups.

Ask a friend to sit in a chair. Be sure your friend has not seen or smelled the liquids you have prepared. Blindfold your friend so he or she cannot see the liquids to be tested. Ask your friend to hold her nose before you hand her a cup that holds a liquid to be tested.

Tell your friend to continue to hold her nose as she takes a small sip of the liquid in the cup. After she has taken a sip, ask her if she can identify the taste of the liquid. Then ask her if she can identify the liquid. Record the results.

Next, have the same subject take a sip of the liquid without holding her nose so that she can smell as well as taste the liquid. Can she identify the taste? Can she identify the liquid? Record the results.

Remove the blindfold and ask your friend to rinse out her mouth with water that she can then spit into a sink before proceeding to the next liquid.

Have your subject taste all the liquids you have prepared. As before, she should be blindfolded. She should first taste the liquid while holding her nose and then with her nose open so that she can smell as well as taste the liquid. Before tasting another liquid, she should rinse her mouth thoroughly with water.

Carry out this experiment with a number of different people, including, if possible, your parents and grandparents. Do you find similar results when you test other people? Do people report less varied tastes when their noses are open rather than closed? Are people better able to identify a liquid when their noses are open rather than closed? Does age seem to affect a person's sense of taste and smell? Are females more or less taste- and smell-sensitive than males? How can you tell?

Exploring on Your Own

Dry your tongue with clean towel. Note the time as you place a few sugar crystals on your tongue. Note the time again when you can taste the sugar. How much time elapsed?

Rinse your mouth thoroughly with water. This time do not dry your mouth before placing a few sugar crystals on it as you note the time. Note the time again when you can taste the sugar. How much time elapsed?

Repeat the same experiment using salt crystals in place of sugar. Again measure the time that elapses before you can taste the salt with both a dry and a moist tongue. What, if anything, can you conclude from your results?

What characteristics must a substance have in order to have a detectable odor? A detectable taste?

4-3
Is It Taste, Texture, or Smell?

We sometimes enjoy the texture of food as well as its flavor. For example, most people prefer to bite into a crisp apple rather than a mealy one. Can similar texture disguise the identity of a food? This experiment will help you to find out.

Prepare some cubes, about a centimeter on a side, from an apple, a potato, a pear, a cucumber, a turnip, and an onion. Then blindfold a friend who has not seen the food.

Ask your blindfolded friend to hold his nose tightly through-

Things you will need:

- apple
- potato
- pear
- cucumber
- turnip
- onion
- blindfold
- a friend
- toothpicks
- notebook
- pen or pencil
- several people of different ages and genders

out the first part of this experiment. As you have seen, closing the nose will greatly reduce your friend's ability to smell the food. Using a toothpick, place one of the small pieces of food on your friend's tongue. Ask him to chew the food and try to identify both the taste and the food. Record his response as well as the actual food being tested. Repeat the experiment with each type of food and record his responses and the actual food being tested in each case.

Next, repeat the experiment with each type of food. But this time have your blindfolded friend chew the small pieces of food with his nose open. Again, record his responses and the actual food being tested in each trial.

Does adding the sense of smell help your friend to identify the food being eaten? Does similarity in texture prevent him from iden-tifying a food when his nose is closed? Does similarity in texture prevent him from identifying a food when his nose is open?

Try the experiment with a number of people of different ages and genders. Are older people less able to identify food than younger people? Does gender make any difference? Do you have any evidence that some people have a stronger sense of smell than others? Do you have any evidence that some people are better able to distinguish foods by texture than others?

4-4*
Smell Fatigue

Have you ever walked into your house when someone was cooking cabbage, broccoli, or a juicy steak? You noticed the odor immediately, but after a while the aroma had faded and you were no longer aware of it. You can experience a similar effect under more controlled conditions.

Things you will need:
- oil of cloves or vanilla extract
- clock or watch with second hand or mode
- perfumes
- vinegar

After noting the time, place your nose about a centimeter above a bottle containing oil of cloves or vanilla extract. Breathe normally through your nose several times. Can you detect the odor of the cloves or vanilla? Now breathe more forcefully, exhaling through your mouth. For how long can you continue to detect the odor?

After you have experienced this particular sensory fatigue (olfactory fatigue), try smelling a different substance, such as perfume or vinegar. Is olfactory fatigue specific to a particular scent, or do you lose your ability to sense all odors for a time?

If you experience olfactory fatigue for a particular perfume, can you still smell a perfume that has a different scent?

After you have recovered from olfactory fatigue, again hold a bottle of oil of cloves or vanilla about a centimeter below your nose. But this time hold one nostril shut so that all the air you breathe enters through one nostril. Continue to inhale through one nostril until you experience olfactory fatigue. Then try inhaling through the other nostril. Can you detect the odor? What does this tell you about the anatomy of your nasal cavity? Is it divided above the nostrils? How do you know?

Now smell a different substance, such as vinegar. Can you detect the odor between sniffs, or only when you are drawing air past the olfactory receptors?

Exploring on Your Own

How does your eye deal with visual fatigue?

Design and carry out experiments to see if sensory fatigue exists for hearing, taste, and touch.

What is anosmia? Can you find anyone who has this disorder? How could you detect it?

4-5*
Threshold of Smell

Some people are more sensitive to smell than others. The minimum amount of a substance that is required for it to be detected by its smell is called the olfactory threshold. In this experiment, you will test yourself and a number of other people to find their olfactory threshold for vanilla.

Things you will need:

- 5 small jars that have screw-on caps
- labels or masking tape
- pen
- graduated cylinder or eyedropper
- several people
- vinegar
- rubbing alcohol
- cooking pan
- stove
- kitchen

You will need to prepare a number of different vanilla solutions. These solutions can be placed in five small jars that have screw-on caps. Label the jars: 1, $\frac{1}{2}$, $\frac{1}{4}$, $\frac{1}{8}$, and $\frac{1}{16}$. To the jar labeled 1 add 20 mL of pure vanilla extract. If you do not have a small graduated cylinder, you can use an eyedropper. One drop is approximately $\frac{1}{20}$ of a milliliter, so 20 drops is equal to a volume of one milliliter. To the jar labeled $\frac{1}{2}$ add 10 mL of vanilla extract and 10 mL of water. This jar has a vanilla concentration that is half that of the first jar because it is mixed with an equal volume of water. The jar labeled $\frac{1}{4}$ should contain 5 mL of vanilla mixed with 15 mL of water. How will you prepare the vanilla solutions in the jars labeled $\frac{1}{8}$ and $\frac{1}{16}$?

Keep the jars tightly capped except when subjects are being tested.

To determine your own olfactory threshold, begin with the least concentrated vanilla solution (the one labeled $\frac{1}{16}$). Can you detect the presence of vanilla by placing the open jar under your nose and sniffing? If you can, your threshold is at a vanilla extract concentration of $\frac{1}{16}$ or less than that of the pure extract.

If you cannot detect the odor of vanilla in that jar, repeat the experiment with the jar labeled ⅛, and, if necessary, continue to test jars of increasing vanilla concentration until you reach your olfactory threshold.

Use the same technique to determine the olfactory threshold for vanilla extract for as many different people as possible. Do people differ significantly in their olfactory thresholds for vanilla?

Repeat the experiment with other substances, such as vinegar and rubbing alcohol. Do the same people who had high olfactory thresholds for vanilla have high thresholds for other substances?

Ask a parent for permission to warm some vanilla extract in a pan so that the kitchen is permeated with the odor of vanilla. How do you think this will affect your olfactory threshold for vanilla? Now test your prediction. Were you right?

Exploring on Your Own

Do adults who smoke cigarettes have a higher olfactory threshold than nonsmokers? Design and carry out an experiment to answer this question.

Taste and Smell Phantoms

How would you like to take a sip of your favorite soda and find that it tasted like vinegar? Or discover that cold water has the same taste as a saturated solution of sugar? Such mysterious changes in taste, known as taste phantoms, are sometimes so bad that a victim of the disorder will refuse to eat. The phenomenon is often associated with a medicine or a viral infection.

The close connection between taste and smell sometimes makes it difficult to tell to which sense a phantom sensation is related. Generally, phantoms that involve sweet, sour, salty, or bitter qualities are disorders related to the nerves that lead to taste buds. People who complain of rotten food, smoke, or gasoline "tastes" are victims of smell phantoms.

People who have taste phantoms often suffer from an intense burning sensation on the tongue known as burning mouth syndrome. Dr. Linda Bartoshuk, a psychologist who specializes in the sense of taste, suggested that both taste phantoms and burning mouth syndrome were the result of damage to a branch of the seventh (VII) cranial nerve that connects with taste buds in the tongue, the chorda tympani. Researchers believe this nerve inhibits taste and pain nerve impulses that arise in the tongue.

Dr. Bartoshuk, together with Dr. John Kveton, found that when they anesthetized the chorda tympani of their subjects, about 40 percent of them experienced taste phantoms. Additional research by Dr. Bartoshuk has shown that subjects with anesthetized chorda tympani also experience increased sensitivity to pain on the tongue. These results indicate that the chorda tympani does indeed inhibit nerve impulses that cause pain and taste phantoms.

Although taste phantoms appear to be consistently related to nerve damage somewhere along the nerve cells connecting tongue and brain, smell phantoms remain a mystery. Some can be explained by injuries or a viral infection, but many appear without any cause that can be identified.

A Dragon with a Keen Scent-Detecting Tongue

The Komodo dragon (*Varanus komodoensis*), found on the Indonesian island of Komodo, is the world's largest and most ferocious lizard. These lizards can grow to a length of 3 meters (10 feet) and weigh 70 kilograms (150 pounds). Their serrated teeth allow them to tear flesh from deer and other animals they devour.

Although these animals can see and hear reasonably well, they detect food primarily by smell. They have a 30-cm (1-foot) yellow, forked tongue that can sense airborne chemicals released by their prey. So sensitive is this organ to molecules carried by the air that the lizard can tell the direction at which its prey is located. If the number of molecules of deer scent reaching the right fork of a dragon's tongue is greater than the number reaching the left fork, this giant lizard knows its next meal is to its right. If it is downwind from carrion, on which it will also feed, it can detect the odor from as far away as 4 kilometers (2.5 miles).

The Komodo dragon is not the animal with a keen sense of smell, although few can match its range. Your pet dog, for example, knows more about the world through his nose than through any other sensory organ. Just watch a dog in new surroundings. It begins by exploring the area with its nose.

Humans do not have a particularly keen sense of smell, but odors are known to be strong memory inducers. This is probably because nerve fibers that respond to odors are directly connected with parts of the brain that store memories.

5

Touch

All our conscious senses consist of receptor cells that respond to stimuli by generating nerve impulses. These impulses are carried by nerve cells to a center in the brain where the impulses are interpreted. It is through our senses that we know what is happening within and outside our bodies.

Cells that respond to light, sound, and the chemical substances that we taste or smell are all located at specific sites in our heads. However, the cells that respond to touch, pain, pressure, and temperature are located in the skin and are spread over most of the body.

Some of the sensations we perceive lead to muscular action. We touch a hot stove and quickly pull our fingers away. We hear a warning and duck! Other sensations, the sounds found in a beautiful piece of music, for example, may elicit pleasant thoughts or memories but no physical response.

Although all sensations are perceived in the brain, we project these sensations to something outside the body or to some part of our body other than our brain. Those sensations that are projected externally include sights, sounds, tastes, smells, touch, temperature, and pressure. Sensations projected internally include pain, balance, hunger, thirst, nausea, fatigue, and a variety of muscular sensations.

Your skin contains receptors that respond to temperature, touch, pressure, and pain. The distribution of these receptors is not even. Some parts of the skin are very sensitive to touch, others are not. Parts of the body most exposed to injury are rich in pain receptors. Strangely, the brain, where pain is perceived, has no pain receptors.

Usually, we can accurately locate pain that arises from injury to the skin. But pain arising in internal organs is often more diffuse. A toothache, for example, may involve the entire side of the face and not just the bad tooth. Pains arising in the heart may seem to be located under the shoulder blades, the muscles of the chest, and in the left shoulder and arm.

5-1
One Touch or Two?

Your skin contains receptors that respond to touch. On some parts of the body, these receptor cells are packed closely together. In other areas of the skin they are far apart.

Things you will need:
- straight pins
- cardboard about 12 cm x 5 cm (4.5 in x 2 in)
- ruler
- a friend
- pencil
- several people
- notebook

The simple device shown in Figure 23 can be used to determine the separation between touch-sensitive cells. Push two straight pins into one side of a piece of cardboard about 12 cm (4.5 in) long and 5 cm (2 in) wide, as shown. Set the heads of the pins about 0.5 cm (0.25 in) apart. Set another set of pins about 1 cm (0.5 in) apart. Set a third set of pins about 2 cm (1.0 in) apart.

Ask a friend to close his or her eyes. Touch the two pins that are closest together gently against the tip on one of your friend's index fingers. Does your friend feel one or two points touching the skin? How close together are the touch receptors on his fingertip?

When you investigate the distance between touch receptors on other parts of the body, be sure you touch areas of the skin that are hairless. To see why, use a pencil to gently push a single hair on your arm. Can you sense that it has been touched? Many hairs have touch receptors near their roots beneath the skin. Can you find any hairs that do not stimulate touch receptors when moved?

Now, again with the pins 0.5 cm (0.25 in) apart, repeat the experiment on other places on the skin. Record your findings in a notebook. **Do not put the pins near anyone's eyes**. You can try other fingertips, the palm of the hand, the back of the hand, different parts of the arm, the lips, ears, and neck, the calf and shin, and the back. Touch the pins to the skin in several places in each area you test.

Next, repeat the tests using the two pins that are 1.0 cm (0.5 in) apart. Can your friend now detect two touch points in regions that were reported as a single point before?

Try the experiment once more with the pinheads 2.0 cm (1.0 in) apart. Can your friend now detect two touch points in regions that were reported as a single point before?

If possible, carry out the experiment with a number of different people. Which parts of the body's skin appear to have the greatest number of touch receptors per area? Which parts have the least?

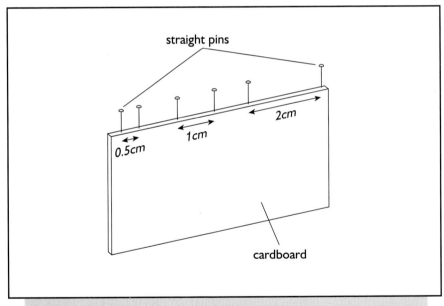

Figure 23. This simple device, made with cardboard and pins, can be used to test for single or multiple touch sensations.

5-2*
Locating Touch

How well can you locate a point on your skin where you have been touched? To find out, use a felt-tipped pen to mark points on a friend's fingertip, palm, wrist, arm, ear, neck, shin, and calf. Ask your friend to close his eyes and hold another felt-tipped pen

Things you will need:
- 2 felt-tipped pens of different color
- a friend
- ballpoint pen
- ruler

of a different color in his dominant hand with his fingers close to the tip. By holding it close to the tip he will minimize any errors resulting from the angle at which the pen is held. Use a ballpoint pen to touch, in turn, each of the colored marks you made before. Immediately after you touch the marked point, have your friend, with his eyes still closed, try to mark the point you have just touched with his colored pen. Measure the separation between the two points. Repeat the experiment at least 5 times to obtain good indications of average error for each location.

Does the location of the touch point on the body affect your friend's ability to identify the point?

How can you measure the average error your friend makes in locating the touch points you established on different parts of his body? Is the average error in locating a touch point related to the ability to recognize two touch points instead of one, as was done in the previous experiment?

It's a Matter of Where You Touch

Pull a few fibers from a cotton swab. Gently drag the fibers across your palm and fingertips. Can you feel anything? Now draw the same fibers gently across your forehead, chin, face, nose, and ear. Can you feel anything in any of these places? What can you conclude?

Can you feel the cotton fibers if you drag them gently along the hairs of your forearm or leg? What can you conclude?

Adaptation

Touch receptors, like receptors that respond to smell, become fatigued through use. Your brain is able to "filter" sensory information and ignore sensory impulses that are not essential to your well-being. As a result, you may become unaware of a touch sensation after a while. To experience this effect, extend your arm with the palm of your hand turned up. Place a cork on the inside of your forearm. How long does it take before you can no longer feel its presence? Does adaptation take longer if the object is heavier?

Pressure

Touch your forearm with the eraser end of a pencil. Then gradually press harder with the pencil. As you press harder, you stimulate receptors deeper in the skin. These receptors respond to pressure. Pressure receptors are the cells that are stimulated when you place a heavy weight on your hand or arm. They enable you to detect the difference between light and heavy objects. Light objects will stimulate touch receptors; heavy objects stimulate pressure receptors. When someone steps on your toe, both pressure and pain receptors are stimulated.

Exploring on Your Own

Carry out an investigation to find out how people who are blind use their sense of touch to read.

5-3*
Touch: A Different Approach

In this experiment you will look more closely at the location of touch receptors. Use a fine-tipped felt pen and a ruler to draw grids, like the one shown in Figure 24, at different places on the skin of a friend. You might draw them on the inside of the lower forearm, back of the

Things you will need:
- fine-tipped felt pen
- ruler
- notebook
- pen or pencil
- broom bristle
- a friend

hand, thumb, palm, cheek, calf, shin, and back. (If hairs are present on any of the skin areas you plan to test, they should be shaved before you draw a grid. Consult an adult about shaving skin.) If the area is small, as on a thumb, use part of the grid. Draw similar grids in your notebook for each on-skin grid you plan to test.

Ask your friend to close her eyes. Using the end of a broom bristle, gently touch the skin within each box of the grid on the back of your friend's hand. Instruct your friend to tell you whenever she feels a touch. For every box on the grid where your friend can feel a touch, use a plus sign (+) to mark the corresponding box on the grid in your notebook. Do not mark boxes in the grid where no touch is felt. Do any boxes within the grid contain more than one touch receptor? If you find more than one receptor within a box, how can you record it?

In how many of the sixteen grid positions did your friend feel touch? About how far apart are the touch receptors on the back of your friend's hand?

Repeat the experiment for other parts of your friend's skin.

Which regions of the body that you tested seem to have the most touch receptors? Which seem to have the fewest touch receptors?

You can use the same grids to look for pain and temperature receptors in the next two experiments.

Exploring on Your Own

Have a subject close her eyes. Then place her finger on a sheet of fine sandpaper. Can she identify what she is touching? Can she identify the sandpaper if you tell her to move her finger along the paper's surface? Are the results different if you use coarse sandpaper? What sensation is produced when the finger moves over the sandpaper that was not present when the finger was at rest?

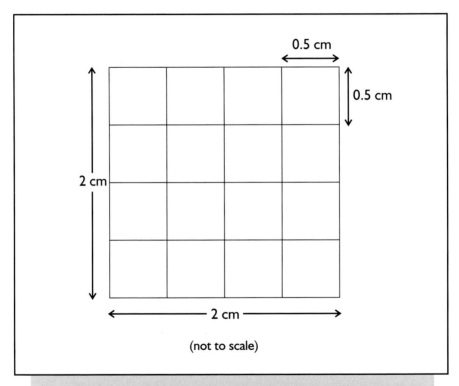

Figure 24. Grids like the one shown here can be drawn on a subject's skin. Touch the center of each box in the grid with the end of a broom bristle. In which of the boxes are touch receptors found in the skin?

5-4
Locating Pain Receptors

Use the same grids on a friend's arm, hand, and so forth that you used in the previous experiment to locate the position of pain receptors within the skin. Again, draw corresponding grids in your notebook so you can record the location of the pain receptors.

Things you will need:

- fine-tipped felt pen
- ruler
- notebook
- pen or pencil
- common pin
- a friend

Ask your friend to close his or her eyes. Then **carefully** use the point of a common pin to touch each box on the skin in the grid. **Do not puncture the skin.** Ask your friend to tell you when he feels any pain. When a pain receptor is found, use a plus (+) sign as before to record its location in your notebook. Leave unmarked those grid boxes where no pain is felt. Do any boxes within the grid contain more than one pain receptor? If you find more than one receptor within a box, how can you record it?

In how many of the sixteen grid positions did your friend feel pain? About how far apart are the pain receptors on the back of your friend's hand?

Which regions of the body that you tested seem to have the most pain receptors? Which seem to have the fewest pain receptors?

5-5*
Locating Receptors Sensitive to Hot and Cold

Use the same grids on a friend's skin that you used in the previous two experiments to locate the position of receptors within the skin that respond to hot or cold temperatures. Again, draw corresponding grids in your notebook so you can record the location of the temperature receptors.

In a washcloth place a finishing nail against an ice cube (see Figure 25). The washcloth will help you to hold the nail firmly against the ice and will also prevent melt water from dripping onto your friend's skin. Heat flows rapidly from a metal; consequently, the end of the nail should not extend very far from the ice.

Things you will need:

- fine-tipped felt pen
- ruler
- notebook
- pen or pencil
- a friend
- finishing nails about 10 cm (4 in) long
- ice cubes
- washcloth
- an adult
- hot water
- teakettle
- stove
- Styrofoam cup
- sink
- oven mitt
- paper towels

Begin by touching the cold metal to grid boxes on your friend's arm. Your friend will tell you whether he feels the cold. In which boxes do you find sensory receptors that respond to cold? Do any boxes within the grid contain more than one receptor sensitive to cold? If you find more than one receptor within a box, how can you record it?

Continue to test using the grids you have drawn on various parts of your friend's body. Where on the body do you find cold receptors are most abundant? On what areas of the body do they seem to be less common?

To test for receptors that respond to heat, you can use similar nails that have been heated. **Ask an adult** to pour hot water from a teakettle into a Styrofoam cup near a sink. Put some 10-cm (4-in) finishing nails, sharp end first, into the hot water. Put on an oven mitt before you remove one of the nails from the hot water. Quickly wipe off any hot water on the nail with a paper towel. Then place the narrow tip of the nail on one of the boxes in a grid on your subject's arm to search for receptors that respond to heat. You will have to put the nail back into the hot water and replace it with another hot nail every few seconds because the nails will cool rapidly.

Continue to search for receptors that respond to warm temperatures on various parts of your friend's body using the grids you have drawn. Your friend will say when he feels the heat of the nail. Where on the body do you find receptors that are sensitive to warm temperatures? Where on the body are these receptors most abundant? On what areas of the body do they seem to be less common?

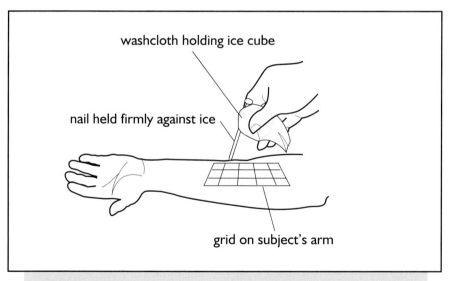

Figure 25. A cold nail can be used to search for receptors sensitive to cold on a subject's skin.

Exploring on Your Own

Design an experiment to determine whether your body adapts (receptors fatigue) more rapidly to touch or to cold.

Is there a temperature range over which your temperature receptors will adapt? If such a range exists, what happens when you exceed the upper or lower limits of that range? Design an experiment to answer these questions. Then, **under adult supervision**, carry out the experiment.

5-6*
Temperature Receptors Are Poor Thermometers

You have found receptors in your skin that respond to hot and cold temperatures. However, as thermometers, these receptors are of poor quality. This experiment, known as the "three bowl experiment," was first carried out by German physiologist Ernst Weber (1795–1878). It will help you to see why temperature receptors are poor thermometers.

Things you will need:

- 3 large bowls
- tap water (hot and cold)
- ice cubes
- clock or watch

To begin, fill one of the three large bowls about three fourths of the way with tap water that is at room temperature. Fill a second bowl about halfway with cold tap water. Add ice cubes until this bowl is also three-fourths full. Fill a third bowl to the same level with hot tap water. Be sure the water is not too hot. If it is, replace some of the water with cold water. You should be able to place your hand in the water without discomfort.

Place the three bowls side by side with the hot water on your right, the ice water on your left, and the room-temperature water in the middle. Dry your hands thoroughly and check the clock. Then place your *right* hand in the hot water and your *left* hand in the ice water. Hold them completely under the water for three minutes.

After three minutes, remove your hands from the bowls and put both of them into the center bowl of room-temperature water. How does the water feel to your *right* hand? How does it feel to your *left* hand? Is it possible for the cool tap water to have two different temperatures at the same time? What does this experiment tell you about the sensory receptors in your skin that respond to temperature?

Exploring on Your Own

If you touch a metallic object and a wooden object, both at room temperature, why will the metal feel cold to touch while the wood will not?

5-7

Weber's Deception: Cold Plus Pressure-Receptor Sensitivity

This experiment is named for German physiologist Ernst Weber, who first discovered this effect. He is the same man who proved that temperature receptors are not good thermometers.

Things you will need:

- a friend
- two 20-gram standard brass masses or two stacks of six pennies glued together
- warm water (40° C, or 105° F) and cup
- ice cube
- several people

Ask a friend to lie on his back on a floor with his eyes closed. On one side of his forehead place a standard 20-gram brass mass that has been in warm water (40° C, or 105° F) for several minutes. On the other side of his forehead place an identical 20-gram brass mass that has been resting on an ice cube for the same length of time. Does your subject believe the two masses are of equal mass or does he think one is heavier than the other? If he does not think they weigh the same, which one does he think is more massive?

Try the same experiment with a number of subjects. Can you offer an explanation for the results you find?

5-8*
Coins to Touch

There is touch and then there is multiple touch. The two can be quite different in terms of the information they provide. To see what this means, put a variety of coins (pennies, nickels, dimes,

Things you will need:

- coins: pennies, nickels, dimes, quarters
- table
- a friend

quarters) in your pocket. Close your eyes and put your hand in your pocket. Turn one of the coins in your fingers and try to identify it. Keeping your eyes closed, remove the coin and place it on a table. Continue this process until you think you have identified and placed on the table at least one coin of each type. Then open your eyes to see how well you have done. You probably did very well.

Now have a friend place the same coins on a table while you stand nearby with your eyes closed. Your friend will guide the tip of your index finger to the top of one of the coins so that you can touch it. Just touch it; do not manipulate it! Can you identify it?

Have your friend guide your finger to other coins. Try to identify the coins just by touching. How well did you do?

Touch alone provides very little information. But by manipulating the coins, you can construct a three-dimensional mental "picture" of the coins that will help you identify them. Just as you could identify coins by feeling them, so people who are blind can "see" a friend by running their hands over that person's face.

Exploring on Your Own

Blindfold a friend and ask her to identify common objects by feeling them with one hand. You might try such things as keys, pens, paper clips, coins, rulers, etc. How accurately can your friend identify items by touch? How well do a number of other people do when given the same task?

List of Suppliers

Carolina Biological Supply Co.
2700 York Road
Burlington, NC 27215
(800) 334-555
http://www.carolina.com

Central Scientific Co. (CENCO)
3300 Cenco Parkway
Franklin Park, IL 60131
(800) 262-3626
http://www.cenconet.com

**Connecticut Valley Biological
Supply Co., Inc.**
82 Valley Road, Box 326
Southampton, MA 01073
(800) 628-7748

Delta Education
P.O. Box 915
Hudson, NH 03051-0915
(800) 258-1302

Edmund Scientific Co.
101 East Gloucester Pike
Barrington, NJ 08007
(609) 547-3488

Educational Innovations, Inc.
151 River Road
Cos Cob, CT 06807-2514
http://www.teachersource.com

Fisher Science Education
485 S. Frontage Road
Burr Ridge, IL 60521
(800) 955–1177
http://www.fisheredu.com

Frey Scientific
100 Paragon Parkway
Mansfield, OH 44903
(800) 225-3739

Nasco-Modesto
P.O. Box 3837
Modesto, CA 95352-3837
(800) 558-9595
http://www.nascofa.com

Nasco-Fort Atkinson
P.O. Box 901
Fort Atkinson, WI 53538-0901
(800) 558-9595

Sargent-Welch/VWR Scientific
P.O. Box 5229
Buffalo Grove, IL 60089-5229
(800) SAR-GENT
http://www.sargentwelch.com

**Science Kit & Boreal
Laboratories**
777 East Park Drive
Tonawanda, NY 14150
(800) 828-7777
http://sciencekit.com

**Ward's Natural Science
Establishment, Inc.**
P.O. Box 92912
Rochester, NY 14692-9012
(800) 962-2660
http://www.wardsci.com

Further Reading

Adams, Richard, and Robert Gardner. *Ideas for Science Projects, Revised Edition.* Danbury, Conn.: Franklin Watts, 1997.

Bochinski, Julianne Blair. *The Complete Handbook of Science Fair Projects.* New York: John Wiley & Sons, 1996.

Bombaugh, Ruth. *Science Fair Success, Revised and Expanded.* Springfield, N.J.: Enslow Publishers, Inc., 1999.

Ciofi, Claudio. "The Komodo Dragon," *Scientific American*, March 1999, pp. 84–91.

Gardner, Robert. *Science Fair Projects—Planning, Presenting, Succeeding.* Springfield, N.J.: Enslow Publishers, Inc., 1999.

————. *Science Projects About the Human Body.* Hillside, N.J.: Enslow Publishers, Inc., 1993.

Goode, Erica. "If Things Taste Bad, 'Phantoms' May Be at Work," *The New York Times*, April 13, 1999.

Hickman, Pamela. *Animal Senses: How Animals See, Hear, Taste, Smell and Feel.* Buffalo, N.Y.: Kids Can Press Ltd., 1998.

The Human Body: An Illustrated Guide to Its Structure, Function, and Disorders. Charles Clayman M.D., editor-in-chief. New York: DK Publishing, 1995.

Krieger, Melanie Jacobs. *How to Excel in Science Competitions, Revised and Updated.* Springfield, N.J: Enslow Publishers, Inc., 1999.

Markle, Sandra. *The Young Scientist's Guide to Successful Science Projects.* New York: Lothrop, Lee, and Shepard, 1990.

Newton, David E. *Making and Using Scientific Equipment.* New York: Franklin Watts, 1993.

Provenzo, Eugene F., and Asterei Baker Provenzo. *47 Easy-to-Do Classic Science Experiments.* New York: Dover, 1989.

Tocci, Salvatore. *How to Do a Science Fair Project, Revised Edition.* Danbury, Conn.: Franklin Watts, 1997.

Van Cleave, Janice. *The Human Body for Every Kid.* New York: John Wiley & Sons, 1995.

Internet Addresses

Chudler, Eric. *Neuroscience for Kids.* © 1996–2000. <http://faculty.washington.edu/chudler/neurok.html> (August 18, 2000).

CyberFair. *Welcome to CyberFair, The Virtual Science Fair.* March 25, 1998. <http://www.isd77.k12.mn.us/resources/cf/> (August 18, 2000).

The Exploratorium. *The Science Explorer.* © 1998. <http://www.exploratorium.edu/science_explorer/> (August 18, 2000).

The Franklin Institute Science Museum. *The Franklin Institute Online.* August 18, 2000. <http://sln.fi.edu> (August 18, 2000).

Los Alamos National Laboratory. *Welcome to Science at Home.* January 26, 2000. <http://education.lanl.gov/> (August 18, 2000).

SciFair.org and John W. Gudenas, Ph.D. *The Ultimate Science Fair Resource.* <http://www.scifair.org> (August 18, 2000).

Index